PERSONAL INFORMATION

Name:

Address:

D1783737

Telephone: Email:

Employer:

Address:

Telephone: Email:

MEDICAL INFORMATION

Physician: Telephone:

Allergies:

Medications:

Blood Type:

Insurer:

IN CASE OF EMERGENCY, NOTIFY

Name:

Address:

Telephone: Relationship:

Published by Barbour Publishing, Inc., 1810 Barbour Drive, Uhrichsville, Ohio 44683, www.barbourbooks.com

Our mission is to inspire the world with the life-changing message of the Bible.

Member of the
Evangelical Christian
Publishers Association

Printed in China.

The LIFE MAP

2022 CREATIVE PLANNER

DAYMAKER

A Division of Barbour Publishing

LOOKING FOR A TOOL TO ORGANIZE YOUR DAYS AND HELP DIRECT YOUR WHOLE LIFE?

This unique planner will help you with the day-to-day, week-to-week, and month-to-month obligations, as well as longer-term goals that will benefit your entire life.

The Life Map 2022 Creative Planner features

- seventeen months' worth of calendars
- a year-at-a-glance section
- pages for frequent contacts
- and more

But the heart of the planner is the monthly emphasis on an important life topic, from the personal and spiritual (such as knowing God more deeply through His Word) to the daily and practical (such as finances, health and wellness, and workplace goals).

This planner offers an important reminder when you aspire to more effective living: God wants to be the center of your plans!

2022

JANUARY

S	M	T	W	T	F	S
						1
2	3	4	5	6	7	8
9	10	11	12	13	14	15
16	17	18	19	20	21	22
23	24	25	26	27	28	29
30	31					

FEBRUARY

S	M	T	W	T	F	S
		1	2	3	4	5
6	7	8	9	10	11	12
13	14	15	16	17	18	19
20	21	22	23	24	25	26
27	28					

MAY

S	M	T	W	T	F	S
1	2	3	4	5	6	7
8	9	10	11	12	13	14
15	16	17	18	19	20	21
22	23	24	25	26	27	28
29	30	31				

JUNE

S	M	T	W	T	F	S
			1	2	3	4
5	6	7	8	9	10	11
12	13	14	15	16	17	18
19	20	21	22	23	24	25
26	27	28	29	30		

SEPTEMBER

S	M	T	W	T	F	S
				1	2	3
4	5	6	7	8	9	10
11	12	13	14	15	16	17
18	19	20	21	22	23	24
25	26	27	28	29	30	

OCTOBER

S	M	T	W	T	F	S
						1
2	3	4	5	6	7	8
9	10	11	12	13	14	15
16	17	18	19	20	21	22
23	24	25	26	27	28	29
30	31					

YEAR at a GLANCE

MARCH

S	M	T	W	T	F	S
		1	2	3	4	5
6	7	8	9	10	11	12
13	14	15	16	17	18	19
20	21	22	23	24	25	26
27	28	29	30	31		

APRIL

S	M	T	W	T	F	S
					1	2
3	4	5	6	7	8	9
10	11	12	13	14	15	16
17	18	19	20	21	22	23
24	25	26	27	28	29	30

JULY

S	M	T	W	T	F	S
					1	2
3	4	5	6	7	8	9
10	11	12	13	14	15	16
17	18	19	20	21	22	23
24	25	26	27	28	29	30
31						

AUGUST

S	M	T	W	T	F	S
	1	2	3	4	5	6
7	8	9	10	11	12	13
14	15	16	17	18	19	20
21	22	23	24	25	26	27
28	29	30	31			

NOVEMBER

S	M	T	W	T	F	S
		1	2	3	4	5
6	7	8	9	10	11	12
13	14	15	16	17	18	19
20	21	22	23	24	25	26
27	28	29	30			

DECEMBER

S	M	T	W	T	F	S
				1	2	3
4	5	6	7	8	9	10
11	12	13	14	15	16	17
18	19	20	21	22	23	24
25	26	27	28	29	30	31

AUGUST 2021

SUNDAY	MONDAY	TUESDAY	WEDNESDAY
1	2	3	4
8	9	10	11
15	16	17	18
22	23	24	25
29	30	31	1

notes

THURSDAY	FRIDAY	SATURDAY
5	6	7
12	13	14
19	20	21
26	27	28
2	3	4

....
....
....
....
....
....
....
....
....
....
....
....
....
....
....

JULY

S	M	T	W	T	F	S
				1	2	3
4	5	6	7	8	9	10
11	12	13	14	15	16	17
18	19	20	21	22	23	24
25	26	27	28	29	30	31

SEPTEMBER

S	M	T	W	T	F	S
			1	2	3	4
5	6	7	8	9	10	11
12	13	14	15	16	17	18
19	20	21	22	23	24	25
26	27	28	29	30		

FAITH BASICS

Fight the good fight of the faith. Take hold of the eternal life to which you were called when you made your good confession in the presence of many witnesses.
1 TIMOTHY 6:12 NIV

God doesn't give us a thousand-dollar gold coin every time we say yes to His Word, His will, and His ways. No, He has something far more valuable reserved for us in heaven. We know this from the words of Jesus, yet do we hold these promises close to our heart? Sometimes. Sometimes not.

Mathematically, *infinity* and *eternity* eclipse seventy-five trillion dollars and a hundred billion light-years. The difference isn't even close. To understand this is paramount to living wisely in our finite, time-bound world. No wonder the apostle Paul calls us to "fight the good fight of the faith" and "take hold of the eternal life to which you were called."

DEAR HEAVENLY FATHER, THANK YOU FOR. . .

HERE'S WHAT'S HAPPENING IN MY LIFE. . .

OTHER THINGS ON MY HEART THAT I NEED TO SHARE WITH YOU, GOD. . .

....
....
....
....
....
....

I need. . .

....
....
....
....
....
....
....

Amen.
Thank You, Father, for hearing my prayers.

GOALS for this MONTH

....
....
....
....
....
....
....

Without faith it is impossible to please God, because anyone who comes to him must believe that he exists and that he rewards those who earnestly seek him.
HEBREWS 11:6 NIV

AUGUST 2021

S	M	T	W	T	F	S
1	2	3	4	5	6	7
8	9	10	11	12	13	14
15	16	17	18	19	20	21
22	23	24	25	26	27	28
29	30	31				

Read the Bible and you soon discover that God likes to call Himself "the Lord God, creator of heaven and earth." He simply spoke and created the whole universe. That realization will change how you see Him (wow!) and how you view creation's greatest hits (awesome!).

to-do list

- [ ]
- [ ]
- [ ]
- [ ]
- [ ]
- [ ]
- [ ]
- [ ]
- [ ]
- [ ]
- [ ]
- [ ]
- [ ]
- [ ]
- [ ]
- [ ]
- [ ]
- [ ]
- [ ]

SUNDAY, AUGUST 1

MONDAY, AUGUST 2

TUESDAY, AUGUST 3

WEDNESDAY, AUGUST 4

THURSDAY, AUGUST 5

FRIDAY, AUGUST 6

SATURDAY, AUGUST 7

to-do list

- [ ]
- [ ]
- [ ]
- [ ]
- [ ]
- [ ]
- [ ]
- [ ]
- [ ]
- [ ]
- [ ]
- [ ]
- [ ]
- [ ]
- [ ]

By faith we understand that the universe was formed at God's command, so that what is seen was not made out of what was visible.
HEBREWS 11:3 NIV

AUGUST 2021

S	M	T	W	T	F	S
1	2	3	4	5	6	7
8	9	10	11	12	13	14
15	16	17	18	19	20	21
22	23	24	25	26	27	28
29	30	31				

No wonder scripture teaches that life is a gift from God—a gift to be cherished and treasured. True, this life is only a small taste of the eternal life to come, but let's make it count!

to-do list

☐ ....
☐ ....
☐ ....
☐ ....
☐ ....
☐ ....
☐ ....
☐ ....
☐ ....
☐ ....
☐ ....
☐ ....
☐ ....
☐ ....
☐ ....
☐ ....
☐ ....
☐ ....
☐ ....

SUNDAY, AUGUST 8

MONDAY, AUGUST 9

TUESDAY, AUGUST 10

WEDNESDAY, AUGUST 11

....
....
....
....

THURSDAY, AUGUST 12

....
....
....
....
....

FRIDAY, AUGUST 13

....
....
....
....
....

SATURDAY, AUGUST 14

....
....
....
....
....

to-do list

- [ ] ....
- [ ] ....
- [ ] ....
- [ ] ....
- [ ] ....
- [ ] ....
- [ ] ....
- [ ] ....
- [ ] ....
- [ ] ....
- [ ] ....
- [ ] ....
- [ ] ....
- [ ] ....
- [ ] ....
- [ ] ....

Then the LORD God formed a man from the dust of the ground and breathed into his nostrils the breath of life, and the man became a living being.
GENESIS 2:7 NIV

AUGUST 2021

S	M	T	W	T	F	S
1	2	3	4	5	6	7
8	9	10	11	12	13	14
15	16	17	18	19	20	21
22	23	24	25	26	27	28
29	30	31				

God stopped walking with Adam and Eve the day they cooled their love and worship for Him. We may be tempted to shake our head and wonder, *How could they?* But let's not forget our own propensity to cool off toward God.

to-do list

- [ ]
- [ ]
- [ ]
- [ ]
- [ ]
- [ ]
- [ ]
- [ ]
- [ ]
- [ ]
- [ ]
- [ ]
- [ ]
- [ ]
- [ ]
- [ ]
- [ ]
- [ ]
- [ ]
- [ ]

SUNDAY, AUGUST 15

MONDAY, AUGUST 16

TUESDAY, AUGUST 17

WEDNESDAY, AUGUST 18

....
....
....
....
....

THURSDAY, AUGUST 19

....
....
....
....
....

FRIDAY, AUGUST 20

....
....
....
....

SATURDAY, AUGUST 21

....
....
....
....
....

to-do list

- ☐ ....
- ☐ ....
- ☐ ....
- ☐ ....
- ☐ ....
- ☐ ....
- ☐ ....
- ☐ ....
- ☐ ....
- ☐ ....
- ☐ ....
- ☐ ....
- ☐ ....
- ☐ ....
- ☐ ....
- ☐ ....
- ☐ ....

But you, man of God,
flee from all this [evil],
and pursue righteousness,
godliness, faith, love,
endurance and gentleness.
1 TIMOTHY 6:11 NIV

AUGUST 2021

S	M	T	W	T	F	S
1	2	3	4	5	6	7
8	9	10	11	12	13	14
15	16	17	18	19	20	21
22	23	24	25	26	27	28
29	30	31				

The more we learn from God's Word (and the more we trust the Lord Himself), the more we will enjoy His good hand of blessing in our lives. Not the "everything goes my way" kind of blessings, but the true gifts: peace with God and others, belonging and significance, hope for the future, and much, much more.

to-do list

- [ ] ....
- [ ] ....
- [ ] ....
- [ ] ....
- [ ] ....
- [ ] ....
- [ ] ....
- [ ] ....
- [ ] ....
- [ ] ....
- [ ] ....
- [ ] ....
- [ ] ....
- [ ] ....
- [ ] ....
- [ ] ....
- [ ] ....
- [ ] ....

SUNDAY, AUGUST 22

MONDAY, AUGUST 23

TUESDAY, AUGUST 24

WEDNESDAY, AUGUST 25

THURSDAY, AUGUST 26

FRIDAY, AUGUST 27

SATURDAY, AUGUST 28

- [ ]
- [ ]
- [ ]
- [ ]
- [ ]
- [ ]
- [ ]
- [ ]
- [ ]
- [ ]
- [ ]
- [ ]
- [ ]
- [ ]
- [ ]
- [ ]
- [ ]

"Receive forgiveness of sins and a place among those who are sanctified by faith in me [Jesus Christ]."
ACTS 26:18 NIV

SEPTEMBER 2021

SUNDAY	MONDAY	TUESDAY	WEDNESDAY
29	30	31	1
5	6 *Labor Day*	7	8
12	13	14	15
19	20	21	22 *First Day of Autumn*
26	27	28	29

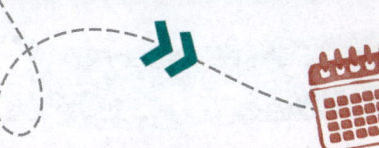

notes

THURSDAY	FRIDAY	SATURDAY
2	3	4
9	10	11
16	17	18
23	24	25
30	1	2

....
....
....
....
....
....
....
....
....
....
....
....
....
....
....
....

AUGUST

S	M	T	W	T	F	S
1	2	3	4	5	6	7
8	9	10	11	12	13	14
15	16	17	18	19	20	21
22	23	24	25	26	27	28
29	30	31				

OCTOBER

S	M	T	W	T	F	S
					1	2
3	4	5	6	7	8	9
10	11	12	13	14	15	16
17	18	19	20	21	22	23
24	25	26	27	28	29	30
31						

BIBLE READING

Jesus answered, "It is written: 'Man shall not live on bread alone, but on every word that comes from the mouth of God.' "
MATTHEW 4:4 NIV

When we read the Bible, we need to do so with our spiritual eyes wide open. How do we do that?

First, go to God in prayer. We can worship God, thank Him for His Word, and ask Him to remove anything that would cloud our hearts and minds as we read the Bible.

Next, ask God for the Holy Spirit's illumination as you read (and reread) each passage of scripture. We can read the same section of the Bible twenty, thirty, or forty times (or more) and still make new discoveries with each reading.

Finally, approach the Bible with a strong sense of expectancy, determination, and persistence. We need to look closely at scripture. The goal of such careful observation is to discover more and more of what God's Word says. We're not conducting a superficial once-over, a cursory glance for some trivial tidbit—we're talking about looking intently at scripture and asking God to change us accordingly.

DEAR HEAVENLY FATHER, THANK YOU FOR. . .

HERE'S WHAT'S HAPPENING IN MY LIFE. . .

OTHER THINGS ON MY HEART THAT
I NEED TO SHARE WITH YOU, GOD. . .

I need. . .

Amen.
Thank You, Father,
for hearing my prayers.

GOALS *for this* MONTH

*I have hidden your word in my heart
that I might not sin against you.*
PSALM 119:11 NIV

SEPTEMBER 2021

S	M	T	W	T	F	S
			1	2	3	4
5	6	7	8	9	10	11
12	13	14	15	16	17	18
19	20	21	22	23	24	25
26	27	28	29	30		

Before we read the Bible each day, there are three essentials. First is reverence for the Lord God, creator of heaven and earth, and the true author of scripture. Second is respect for the Bible itself. Third is repentance of any known sin in our lives. We want the author of scripture to speak to us freely.

to-do list

- [ ] ....
- [ ] ....
- [ ] ....
- [ ] ....
- [ ] ....
- [ ] ....
- [ ] ....
- [ ] ....
- [ ] ....
- [ ] ....
- [ ] ....
- [ ] ....
- [ ] ....
- [ ] ....
- [ ] ....
- [ ] ....
- [ ] ....
- [ ] ....

SUNDAY, AUGUST 29

MONDAY, AUGUST 30

TUESDAY, AUGUST 31

WEDNESDAY, SEPTEMBER 1

....
....
....
....
....

THURSDAY, SEPTEMBER 2

....
....
....
....
....

FRIDAY, SEPTEMBER 3

....
....
....
....
....

SATURDAY, SEPTEMBER 4

....
....
....
....
....

to-do list

☐ ....
☐ ....
☐ ....
☐ ....
☐ ....
☐ ....
☐ ....
☐ ....
☐ ....
☐ ....
☐ ....
☐ ....
☐ ....
☐ ....
☐ ....
☐ ....

"I have not departed from the commands of [God's] lips; I have treasured the words of his mouth more than my daily bread."
JOB 23:12 NIV

SEPTEMBER 2021

S	M	T	W	T	F	S
				1	2	3	4
5	6	7	8	9	10	11
12	13	14	15	16	17	18
19	20	21	22	23	24	25
26	27	28	29	30		

When you read the Bible, read to learn—and read to be moved emotionally. If your emotions are engaged, you'll remember what you read for months and years and decades to come.

to-do list

- ☐ ....
- ☐ ....
- ☐ ....
- ☐ ....
- ☐ ....
- ☐ ....
- ☐ ....
- ☐ ....
- ☐ ....
- ☐ ....
- ☐ ....
- ☐ ....
- ☐ ....
- ☐ ....
- ☐ ....
- ☐ ....
- ☐ ....
- ☐ ....
- ☐ ....

SUNDAY, SEPTEMBER 5

MONDAY, SEPTEMBER 6 — Labor Day

TUESDAY, SEPTEMBER 7

WEDNESDAY, SEPTEMBER 8

THURSDAY, SEPTEMBER 9

FRIDAY, SEPTEMBER 10

SATURDAY, SEPTEMBER 11

to-do list

- [ ]
- [ ]
- [ ]
- [ ]
- [ ]
- [ ]
- [ ]
- [ ]
- [ ]
- [ ]
- [ ]
- [ ]
- [ ]
- [ ]
- [ ]
- [ ]
- [ ]

They read from the Book of the Law of God, making it clear and giving the meaning so that the people understood what was being read.
NEHEMIAH 8:8 NIV

SEPTEMBER 2021

S	M	T	W	T	F	S
			1	2	3	4
5	6	7	8	9	10	11
12	13	14	15	16	17	18
19	20	21	22	23	24	25
26	27	28	29	30		

Read scripture with your head *and* heart. If you don't understand something, it's okay to ask questions. But as you read, focus on what is clear. Look for (1) examples to heed, (2) truths to believe, and (3) commands to obey.

to-do list

- [ ]
- [ ]
- [ ]
- [ ]
- [ ]
- [ ]
- [ ]
- [ ]
- [ ]
- [ ]
- [ ]
- [ ]
- [ ]
- [ ]
- [ ]
- [ ]
- [ ]
- [ ]

SUNDAY, SEPTEMBER 12

MONDAY, SEPTEMBER 13

TUESDAY, SEPTEMBER 14

WEDNESDAY, SEPTEMBER 15

THURSDAY, SEPTEMBER 16

FRIDAY, SEPTEMBER 17

SATURDAY, SEPTEMBER 18

to-do list

- [ ]
- [ ]
- [ ]
- [ ]
- [ ]
- [ ]
- [ ]
- [ ]
- [ ]
- [ ]
- [ ]
- [ ]
- [ ]
- [ ]
- [ ]
- [ ]

*So then faith comes
by hearing, and hearing
by the word of God.*
ROMANS 10:17 NKJV

SEPTEMBER 2021

S	M	T	W	T	F	S
			1	2	3	4
5	6	7	8	9	10	11
12	13	14	15	16	17	18
19	20	21	22	23	24	25
26	27	28	29	30		

The Bible is full of truths, but some have greater impact on our lives. The most important ones teach realities about the Lord God. The more we know and affirm them, the greater He will bless our lives.

to-do list

- [ ]
- [ ]
- [ ]
- [ ]
- [ ]
- [ ]
- [ ]
- [ ]
- [ ]
- [ ]
- [ ]
- [ ]
- [ ]
- [ ]
- [ ]
- [ ]
- [ ]
- [ ]

SUNDAY, SEPTEMBER 19

MONDAY, SEPTEMBER 20

TUESDAY, SEPTEMBER 21

WEDNESDAY, SEPTEMBER 22
First Day of Autumn

THURSDAY, SEPTEMBER 23

FRIDAY, SEPTEMBER 24

SATURDAY, SEPTEMBER 25

to-do list

☐
☐
☐
☐
☐
☐
☐
☐
☐
☐
☐
☐
☐
☐
☐
☐

For the word of God is alive and active. Sharper than any double-edged sword, it penetrates even to dividing soul and spirit, joints and marrow; it judges the thoughts and attitudes of the heart.
HEBREWS 4:12 NIV

SEPTEMBER 2021

S	M	T	W	T	F	S
				1	2	3	4
5	6	7	8	9	10	11
12	13	14	15	16	17	18
19	20	21	22	23	24	25
26	27	28	29	30		

When we come to the Lord to pray for ourselves, we must first experience ourselves as He does. Do you imagine that God hears you as a bothersome interruption or an unwelcome visitor? If so, you will hesitate to go to Him with your needs, hurts, and deepest desires. If you know that you are God's beloved child, you'll trust that He hears your voice with delight.

to-do list

- [ ]
- [ ]
- [ ]
- [ ]
- [ ]
- [ ]
- [ ]
- [ ]
- [ ]
- [ ]
- [ ]
- [ ]
- [ ]
- [ ]
- [ ]
- [ ]
- [ ]
- [ ]

SUNDAY, SEPTEMBER 26

MONDAY, SEPTEMBER 27

TUESDAY, SEPTEMBER 28

WEDNESDAY, SEPTEMBER 29

THURSDAY, SEPTEMBER 30

FRIDAY, OCTOBER 1

SATURDAY, OCTOBER 2

- [ ]
- [ ]
- [ ]
- [ ]
- [ ]
- [ ]
- [ ]
- [ ]
- [ ]
- [ ]
- [ ]
- [ ]
- [ ]
- [ ]
- [ ]
- [ ]

"The Father himself loves you dearly because you love me [Jesus] and believe that I came from God."
JOHN 16:27 NLT

OCTOBER 2021

SUNDAY	MONDAY	TUESDAY	WEDNESDAY
26	27	28	29
3	4	5	6
10	11 *Columbus Day*	12	13
17	18	19	20
24	25	26	27
31 *Halloween*			

notes

THURSDAY	FRIDAY	SATURDAY
30	1	2
7	8	9
14	15	16
21	22	23
28	29	30

....
....
....
....
....
....
....
....
....
....
....
....
....

SEPTEMBER

S	M	T	W	T	F	S
			1	2	3	4
5	6	7	8	9	10	11
12	13	14	15	16	17	18
19	20	21	22	23	24	25
26	27	28	29	30		

NOVEMBER

S	M	T	W	T	F	S
	1	2	3	4	5	6
7	8	9	10	11	12	13
14	15	16	17	18	19	20
21	22	23	24	25	26	27
28	29	30				

PRAYER

"Ask and it will be given to you; seek and you will find;
knock and the door will be opened to you."
MATTHEW 7:7 NIV

Does it seem selfish to pray for yourself? We may choose to pray often for others (which is great!) but feel less comfortable talking to God about our own needs. But that is appropriate prayer too.

God repeatedly invites us to ask Him for things we need. Jesus asked people, "What do you want me to do for you?" In fact, *not* asking is wrong. God was angry with King Ahab when he refused to ask for anything (Isaiah 7:10–14). When King Asa refused to pray about his own serious illness, he died (2 Chronicles 16:12). In both cases, their blatant unwillingness to pray revealed a lack of love for God, and failure to trust Him.

Yes, we will experience God's power answering our prayers for *other* people, but He also wants us to experience His power to answer *our* prayers, meet *our* needs, and change *our* lives.

DEAR HEAVENLY FATHER, THANK YOU FOR. . .

HERE'S WHAT'S HAPPENING IN MY LIFE. . .

OTHER THINGS ON MY HEART THAT I NEED TO SHARE WITH YOU, GOD. . .

I need. . .

Amen.

Thank You, Father,
for hearing my prayers.

GOALS *for this* MONTH

*"What do you want me to do for you?" Jesus asked him.
The blind man said, "Rabbi, I want to see."*
MARK 10:51 NIV

OCTOBER 2021

S	M	T	W	T	F	S
					1	2
3	4	5	6	7	8	9
10	11	12	13	14	15	16
17	18	19	20	21	22	23
24	25	26	27	28	29	30
31						

When you pray for yourself, you can bare your soul completely to God. God can handle any emotions you're experiencing and any questions you bring. He isn't uneasy or afraid or caught off guard.

to-do list

- [ ]
- [ ]
- [ ]
- [ ]
- [ ]
- [ ]
- [ ]
- [ ]
- [ ]
- [ ]
- [ ]
- [ ]
- [ ]
- [ ]
- [ ]
- [ ]
- [ ]
- [ ]
- [ ]

SUNDAY, OCTOBER 3

MONDAY, OCTOBER 4

TUESDAY, OCTOBER 5

WEDNESDAY, OCTOBER 6

....
....
....
....
....

THURSDAY, OCTOBER 7

....
....
....
....
....

FRIDAY, OCTOBER 8

....
....
....
....
....

SATURDAY, OCTOBER 9

....
....
....
....
....

to-do list

- [ ] ....
- [ ] ....
- [ ] ....
- [ ] ....
- [ ] ....
- [ ] ....
- [ ] ....
- [ ] ....
- [ ] ....
- [ ] ....
- [ ] ....
- [ ] ....
- [ ] ....
- [ ] ....
- [ ] ....
- [ ] ....

*I cry out to the LORD;
I plead for the LORD's
mercy. I pour out my
complaints before him
and tell him all my troubles.*
PSALM 142:1–2 NLT

OCTOBER 2021

S	M	T	W	T	F	S
					1	2
3	4	5	6	7	8	9
10	11	12	13	14	15	16
17	18	19	20	21	22	23
24	25	26	27	28	29	30
31						

Praying for ourselves starts best with introspection. We ask God to forgive us not only for our daily sins but also for the patterns of disobedience, unkindness, or selfishness in our lives. We ask the Holy Spirit to reveal these to us and to change us from the inside out.

to-do list

- [ ]
- [ ]
- [ ]
- [ ]
- [ ]
- [ ]
- [ ]
- [ ]
- [ ]
- [ ]
- [ ]
- [ ]
- [ ]
- [ ]
- [ ]
- [ ]
- [ ]
- [ ]

SUNDAY, OCTOBER 10

MONDAY, OCTOBER 11 *Columbus Day*

TUESDAY, OCTOBER 12

WEDNESDAY, OCTOBER 13

THURSDAY, OCTOBER 14

FRIDAY, OCTOBER 15

SATURDAY, OCTOBER 16

to-do list

☐
☐
☐
☐
☐
☐
☐
☐
☐
☐
☐
☐
☐
☐
☐
☐

Search me, God, and know my heart; test me and know my anxious thoughts. See if there is any offensive way in me, and lead me in the way everlasting.
PSALM 139:23–24 NIV

OCTOBER 2021

S	M	T	W	T	F	S
					1	2
3	4	5	6	7	8	9
10	11	12	13	14	15	16
17	18	19	20	21	22	23
24	25	26	27	28	29	30
31						

How often have you lain awake at night, your mind swirling with anxiety and your spirit crushed with depression? During such times, fill your mind with worship for who God is and thankfulness for what He's done. Have a verse ready to recite, "Rejoice in the Lord always; again I will say, rejoice" (Philippians 4:4 ESV) or "Don't worry about anything; instead, pray about everything" (Philippians 4:6 NLT).

to-do list

- [ ]
- [ ]
- [ ]
- [ ]
- [ ]
- [ ]
- [ ]
- [ ]
- [ ]
- [ ]
- [ ]
- [ ]
- [ ]
- [ ]
- [ ]
- [ ]
- [ ]
- [ ]

SUNDAY, OCTOBER 17

MONDAY, OCTOBER 18

TUESDAY, OCTOBER 19

WEDNESDAY, OCTOBER 20

THURSDAY, OCTOBER 21

FRIDAY, OCTOBER 22

SATURDAY, OCTOBER 23

- [ ]
- [ ]
- [ ]
- [ ]
- [ ]
- [ ]
- [ ]
- [ ]
- [ ]
- [ ]
- [ ]
- [ ]
- [ ]
- [ ]
- [ ]
- [ ]

*Enter his gates with
thanksgiving, and his
courts with praise!
Give thanks to him;
bless his name!*
PSALM 100:4 ESV

OCTOBER 2021

S	M	T	W	T	F	S
					1	2
3	4	5	6	7	8	9
10	11	12	13	14	15	16
17	18	19	20	21	22	23
24	25	26	27	28	29	30
31						

You've walked through God's gates with thanksgiving. You've prayed for the Lord to search your heart. You've asked Him to change you from the inside out. What else is on your heart and mind? Ask the Lord to respond to each concern in a specific, detailed manner. Then watch for His answers. Don't rush by and miss them!

to-do list

- [ ]
- [ ]
- [ ]
- [ ]
- [ ]
- [ ]
- [ ]
- [ ]
- [ ]
- [ ]
- [ ]
- [ ]
- [ ]
- [ ]
- [ ]
- [ ]
- [ ]
- [ ]
- [ ]

SUNDAY, OCTOBER 24

MONDAY, OCTOBER 25

TUESDAY, OCTOBER 26

WEDNESDAY, OCTOBER 27

THURSDAY, OCTOBER 28

FRIDAY, OCTOBER 29

SATURDAY, OCTOBER 30

☐
☐
☐
☐
☐
☐
☐
☐
☐
☐
☐
☐
☐
☐
☐
☐

*"Then you will know
that I am the LORD;
those who hope in me
will not be disappointed."*
ISAIAH 49:23 NIV

NOVEMBER 2021

SUNDAY	MONDAY	TUESDAY	WEDNESDAY
31	1	2 *Election Day*	3
7 *Daylight Saving Time Ends*	8	9	10
14	15	16	17
21	22	23	24
28 *Hanukkah Begins at Sundown*	29	30	1

notes

THURSDAY	FRIDAY	SATURDAY
4	5	6
11 *Veterans Day*	12	13
18	19	20
25 *Thanksgiving Day*	26	27
2	3	4

....
....
....
....
....
....
....
....
....
....
....
....
....
....
....

OCTOBER

S	M	T	W	T	F	S
					1	2
3	4	5	6	7	8	9
10	11	12	13	14	15	16
17	18	19	20	21	22	23
24	25	26	27	28	29	30
31						

DECEMBER

S	M	T	W	T	F	S
			1	2	3	4
5	6	7	8	9	10	11
12	13	14	15	16	17	18
19	20	21	22	23	24	25
26	27	28	29	30	31	

HOSPITALITY

When [Lydia] and the members of her household were baptized,
she invited us to her home. "If you consider me a believer in the Lord,"
she said, "come and stay at my house." And she persuaded us.
ACTS 16:15 NIV

How important is hospitality in your home?

Down through the ages, in most cultures around the world, eating meals together has been the fabric of life. It's how life is lived within families, neighborhoods, and other spheres of relationship. We certainly see this in the lives of the biblical heroes of the faith as well as the ancient Jewish people. The latter celebrated Sabbath meals, other religious get-togethers, and at least three multiday national festivals each year.

Jesus and His apostles ate together often, as did the early believers who followed them. They also invited a wide assortment of other people to join in.

Hospitality is an expected part of each Christian's character and way of life. Let's make it a bigger part of our lives this holiday season.

DEAR HEAVENLY FATHER, THANK YOU FOR. . .

HERE'S WHAT'S HAPPENING IN MY LIFE. . .

OTHER THINGS ON MY HEART THAT I NEED TO SHARE WITH YOU, GOD. . .

I need. . .

Amen.

Thank You, Father,
for hearing my prayers.

GOALS *for this* MONTH

*While Jesus was having dinner at Matthew's house,
many tax collectors and sinners came and
ate with him and his disciples.*
MATTHEW 9:10 NIV

NOVEMBER 2021

S	M	T	W	T	F	S
		1	2	3	4	5	6
7	8	9	10	11	12	13
14	15	16	17	18	19	20
21	22	23	24	25	26	27
28	29	30				

Some people love meeting new people, but most of us prefer to stick to the friends we know, especially when it comes to sharing our time and homes. Jesus, though, bluntly told us to invite the uninvited. In the verse below, that means people whose income level or disability keeps them out of regular social circles.

to-do list

- [ ] ....
- [ ] ....
- [ ] ....
- [ ] ....
- [ ] ....
- [ ] ....
- [ ] ....
- [ ] ....
- [ ] ....
- [ ] ....
- [ ] ....
- [ ] ....
- [ ] ....
- [ ] ....
- [ ] ....
- [ ] ....
- [ ] ....

SUNDAY, OCTOBER 31 — *Halloween*

MONDAY, NOVEMBER 1

TUESDAY, NOVEMBER 2 — *Election Day*

WEDNESDAY, NOVEMBER 3

....
....
....
....
....

THURSDAY, NOVEMBER 4

....
....
....
....
....

FRIDAY, NOVEMBER 5

....
....
....
....
....

SATURDAY, NOVEMBER 6

....
....
....
....
....

to-do list

- ☐ ....
- ☐ ....
- ☐ ....
- ☐ ....
- ☐ ....
- ☐ ....
- ☐ ....
- ☐ ....
- ☐ ....
- ☐ ....
- ☐ ....
- ☐ ....
- ☐ ....
- ☐ ....
- ☐ ....
- ☐ ....

But when you give a banquet, invite. . .the crippled, the lame, the blind.
LUKE 14:13 NIV

NOVEMBER 2021

S	M	T	W	T	F	S
	1	2	3	4	5	6
7	8	9	10	11	12	13
14	15	16	17	18	19	20
21	22	23	24	25	26	27
28	29	30				

You probably know people who struggle financially. Make sure to include them on the guest lists of your holiday parties. Get to know them. Find out where they come from and what they enjoy. Be unshockable if they reveal what they lack—and be ready with cash to quietly meet at least one specific need. The Lord promises to reward you.

to-do list

- [ ]
- [ ]
- [ ]
- [ ]
- [ ]
- [ ]
- [ ]
- [ ]
- [ ]
- [ ]
- [ ]
- [ ]
- [ ]
- [ ]
- [ ]
- [ ]
- [ ]
- [ ]

SUNDAY, NOVEMBER 7
Daylight Saving Time Ends

MONDAY, NOVEMBER 8

TUESDAY, NOVEMBER 9

WEDNESDAY, NOVEMBER 10

THURSDAY, NOVEMBER 11
Veterans Day

FRIDAY, NOVEMBER 12

SATURDAY, NOVEMBER 13

to-do list

- [ ]
- [ ]
- [ ]
- [ ]
- [ ]
- [ ]
- [ ]
- [ ]
- [ ]
- [ ]
- [ ]
- [ ]
- [ ]
- [ ]
- [ ]
- [ ]
- [ ]

And do not forget to do good and to share with others, for with such sacrifices God is pleased.
HEBREWS 13:16 NIV

NOVEMBER 2021

S	M	T	W	T	F	S
	1	2	3	4	5	6
7	8	9	10	11	12	13
14	15	16	17	18	19	20
21	22	23	24	25	26	27
28	29	30				

Think about the physical layout of your home, both inside and out. Ask your disabled friends if it's manageable. If so, invite them to join you for dinner. When they arrive, simply offer an arm or a hand. If they take it, great! If not, let them manage on their own. Dinner at your home will probably be the highlight of their week—and yours.

to-do list

☐
☐
☐
☐
☐
☐
☐
☐
☐
☐
☐
☐
☐
☐
☐
☐
☐
☐
☐

SUNDAY, NOVEMBER 14

MONDAY, NOVEMBER 15

TUESDAY, NOVEMBER 16

WEDNESDAY, NOVEMBER 17

THURSDAY, NOVEMBER 18

FRIDAY, NOVEMBER 19

SATURDAY, NOVEMBER 20

to-do list

And Mephibosheth,
who was crippled in
both feet, lived in
Jerusalem and ate
regularly at the
king's table.
2 SAMUEL 9:13 NLT

NOVEMBER 2021

S	M	T	W	T	F	S
		1	2	3	4	5	6
7	8	9	10	11	12	13
14	15	16	17	18	19	20
21	22	23	24	25	26	27
28	29	30				

Consider the impoverished immigrants in your community, often working two or three jobs to make do. They need a friend like you. Invite them over and accept their invitations in return. Discover what they need, and do what you can to help. Always the greater blessing is yours.

to-do list

- [ ]
- [ ]
- [ ]
- [ ]
- [ ]
- [ ]
- [ ]
- [ ]
- [ ]
- [ ]
- [ ]
- [ ]
- [ ]
- [ ]
- [ ]
- [ ]
- [ ]
- [ ]

SUNDAY, NOVEMBER 21

MONDAY, NOVEMBER 22

TUESDAY, NOVEMBER 23

WEDNESDAY, NOVEMBER 24

....
....
....
....
....

THURSDAY, NOVEMBER 25
Thanksgiving Day

....
....
....
....

FRIDAY, NOVEMBER 26

....
....
....
....
....

SATURDAY, NOVEMBER 27

....
....
....
....
....

to-do list

☐ ....
☐ ....
☐ ....
☐ ....
☐ ....
☐ ....
☐ ....
☐ ....
☐ ....
☐ ....
☐ ....
☐ ....
☐ ....
☐ ....
☐ ....

*He defends the cause of the
fatherless and the widow,
and loves the foreigner
residing among you, giving
them food and clothing.*
DEUTERONOMY 10:18 NIV

DECEMBER 2021

SUNDAY	MONDAY	TUESDAY	WEDNESDAY
28	29	30	1
5	6	7	8
12	13	14	15
19	20	21 *First Day of Winter*	22
26	27	28	29

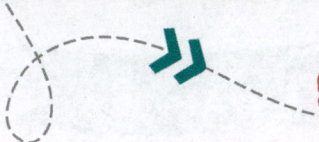

notes

THURSDAY	FRIDAY	SATURDAY
2	3	4
9	10	11
16	17	18
23	24 *Christmas Eve*	25 *Christmas Day*
30	31 *New Year's Eve*	1

....
....
....
....
....
....
....
....
....
....
....

NOVEMBER

S	M	T	W	T	F	S
	1	2	3	4	5	6
7	8	9	10	11	12	13
14	15	16	17	18	19	20
21	22	23	24	25	26	27
28	29	30				

JANUARY

S	M	T	W	T	F	S
						1
2	3	4	5	6	7	8
9	10	11	12	13	14	15
16	17	18	19	20	21	22
23	24	25	26	27	28	29
30	31					

GOD'S WILL

He has told you, O man, what is good; and what
does the LORD require of you but to do justice, and to
love kindness, and to walk humbly with your God?
MICAH 6:8 ESV

God's will is sometimes less exciting than we might wish. Consider one man's story:

War had broken out, and the future of nations was at stake. Huge shipments of bullets arrived daily in a certain lab, where one specimen from each load was tested to ensure quality. The man in charge of the testing couldn't have been more qualified for the job—he was a true master. But a burning patriotism fueled his desire to be on the front lines. Finally, he received his orders and went to the battle zone where, within a short time, he was gunned down by the enemy.

How tragic that this man couldn't see the tremendous significance of his behind-the-scenes contributions to the war effort!

Most of God's will is less than exciting. That's true of many of our responsibilities, on the job, at church, or in our home. But God doesn't call us to pursue what's thrilling—He calls us to persevere in doing His will.

DEAR HEAVENLY FATHER, THANK YOU FOR. . .

HERE'S WHAT'S HAPPENING IN MY LIFE. . .

OTHER THINGS ON MY HEART THAT
I NEED TO SHARE WITH YOU, GOD. . .

....

....

....

....

....

....

I need. . .

....

....

....

....

....

....

Amen.
Thank You, Father,
for hearing my prayers.

GOALS *for this* MONTH

....

....

....

....

....

....

....

....

*You need to persevere so that when you have done the
will of God, you will receive what he has promised.*
HEBREWS 10:36 NIV

DECEMBER 2021

S	M	T	W	T	F	S
			1	2	3	4
5	6	7	8	9	10	11
12	13	14	15	16	17	18
19	20	21	22	23	24	25
26	27	28	29	30	31	

Brother Lawrence, the seventeenth-century monk who wrote *The Practice of the Presence of God*, once said, "We ought not to be weary of doing little things for the love of God, who regards not the greatness of the work, but the love with which it is performed."

to-do list

- [ ]
- [ ]
- [ ]
- [ ]
- [ ]
- [ ]
- [ ]
- [ ]
- [ ]
- [ ]
- [ ]
- [ ]
- [ ]
- [ ]
- [ ]
- [ ]
- [ ]
- [ ]
- [ ]

SUNDAY, NOVEMBER 28
Hanukkah Begins at Sundown

MONDAY, NOVEMBER 29

TUESDAY, NOVEMBER 30

WEDNESDAY, DECEMBER 1

....

....

....

....

....

THURSDAY, DECEMBER 2

....

....

....

....

....

FRIDAY, DECEMBER 3

....

....

....

....

....

SATURDAY, DECEMBER 4

....

....

....

....

....

to-do list

- [ ] ....
- [ ] ....
- [ ] ....
- [ ] ....
- [ ] ....
- [ ] ....
- [ ] ....
- [ ] ....
- [ ] ....
- [ ] ....
- [ ] ....
- [ ] ....
- [ ] ....
- [ ] ....
- [ ] ....
- [ ] ....

"But seek first [God's] kingdom and his righteousness, and all these things will be given to you as well."
MATTHEW 6:33 NIV

DECEMBER 2021

S	M	T	W	T	F	S
			1	2	3	4
5	6	7	8	9	10	11
12	13	14	15	16	17	18
19	20	21	22	23	24	25
26	27	28	29	30	31	

When the Lord called Joshua to march around Jericho for seven days, He didn't explain why. God simply said that He was the supreme commander and ordered Joshua to remove his sandals. Ordinary sand can become holy ground. Joshua obeyed and accomplished great things. So can we.

to-do list

- [ ] ....
- [ ] ....
- [ ] ....
- [ ] ....
- [ ] ....
- [ ] ....
- [ ] ....
- [ ] ....
- [ ] ....
- [ ] ....
- [ ] ....
- [ ] ....
- [ ] ....
- [ ] ....
- [ ] ....
- [ ] ....
- [ ] ....
- [ ] ....
- [ ] ....

SUNDAY, DECEMBER 5

MONDAY, DECEMBER 6

TUESDAY, DECEMBER 7

WEDNESDAY, DECEMBER 8

THURSDAY, DECEMBER 9

FRIDAY, DECEMBER 10

SATURDAY, DECEMBER 11

to-do list

☐
☐
☐
☐
☐
☐
☐
☐
☐
☐
☐
☐
☐
☐
☐
☐

And we know that in all things God works for the good of those who love him, who have been called according to his purpose.
ROMANS 8:28 NIV

DECEMBER 2021

S	M	T	W	T	F	S
			1	2	3	4
5	6	7	8	9	10	11
12	13	14	15	16	17	18
19	20	21	22	23	24	25
26	27	28	29	30	31	

In the Bible we sometimes find God telling Noah, Abraham, Joseph, Joshua, and other main characters what to do. But it's rare for God to speak to us so directly. That's why it's so important to know and apply key biblical principles about His will.

to-do list

- [ ] ....
- [ ] ....
- [ ] ....
- [ ] ....
- [ ] ....
- [ ] ....
- [ ] ....
- [ ] ....
- [ ] ....
- [ ] ....
- [ ] ....
- [ ] ....
- [ ] ....
- [ ] ....
- [ ] ....
- [ ] ....
- [ ] ....
- [ ] ....

SUNDAY, DECEMBER 12

MONDAY, DECEMBER 13

TUESDAY, DECEMBER 14

WEDNESDAY, DECEMBER 15

....
....
....
....
....

THURSDAY, DECEMBER 16

....
....
....
....
....

FRIDAY, DECEMBER 17

....
....
....
....
....

SATURDAY, DECEMBER 18

....
....
....
....
....

to-do list

☐ ....
☐ ....
☐ ....
☐ ....
☐ ....
☐ ....
☐ ....
☐ ....
☐ ....
☐ ....
☐ ....
☐ ....
☐ ....
☐ ....
☐ ....
☐ ....
☐ ....

*Be thankful in all
circumstances, for this
is God's will for you who
belong to Christ Jesus.*
1 THESSALONIANS 5:18 NLT

DECEMBER 2021

S	M	T	W	T	F	S
				1	2	3	4
5	6	7	8	9	10	11
12	13	14	15	16	17	18
19	20	21	22	23	24	25
26	27	28	29	30	31	

God's will often takes much longer than we expect. Sadly, many of us fail in God's waiting rooms. Why? Here is one key reason: We keep our eyes on other people. Ask yourself, "What difference would it make if I didn't care what everyone else thought?"

to-do list

☐ ....
☐ ....
☐ ....
☐ ....
☐ ....
☐ ....
☐ ....
☐ ....
☐ ....
☐ ....
☐ ....
☐ ....
☐ ....
☐ ....
☐ ....
☐ ....
☐ ....
☐ ....
☐ ....

SUNDAY, DECEMBER 19

MONDAY, DECEMBER 20

TUESDAY, DECEMBER 21
First Day of Winter

WEDNESDAY, DECEMBER 22

THURSDAY, DECEMBER 23

FRIDAY, DECEMBER 24   *Christmas Eve*

SATURDAY, DECEMBER 25
Christmas Day

to-do list

- [ ]
- [ ]
- [ ]
- [ ]
- [ ]
- [ ]
- [ ]
- [ ]
- [ ]
- [ ]
- [ ]
- [ ]
- [ ]
- [ ]
- [ ]
- [ ]

Now may the God of peace. . .equip you with everything good for doing his will, and may he work in us what is pleasing to him, through Jesus Christ, to whom be glory for ever and ever. Amen.
HEBREWS 13:20–21 NIV

DECEMBER 2021

S	M	T	W	T	F	S
			1	2	3	4
5	6	7	8	9	10	11
12	13	14	15	16	17	18
19	20	21	22	23	24	25
26	27	28	29	30	31	

Let's truly seek God's will day in and day out. Let's maintain an eternal perspective. After all, we have a very long time to celebrate our victories.

to-do list

- [ ]
- [ ]
- [ ]
- [ ]
- [ ]
- [ ]
- [ ]
- [ ]
- [ ]
- [ ]
- [ ]
- [ ]
- [ ]
- [ ]
- [ ]
- [ ]
- [ ]
- [ ]
- [ ]

SUNDAY, DECEMBER 26

MONDAY, DECEMBER 27

TUESDAY, DECEMBER 28

WEDNESDAY, DECEMBER 29

....
....
....
....
....

THURSDAY, DECEMBER 30

....
....
....
....
....

FRIDAY, DECEMBER 31 *New Year's Eve*

....
....
....
....
....

SATURDAY, JANUARY 1 *New Year's Day*

....
....
....
....
....

to-do list

☐ ....
☐ ....
☐ ....
☐ ....
☐ ....
☐ ....
☐ ....
☐ ....
☐ ....
☐ ....
☐ ....
☐ ....
☐ ....
☐ ....
☐ ....
☐ ....

"This, then, is how you
should pray: 'Our Father
in heaven, hallowed be
your name, your kingdom
come, your will be done,
on earth as it is in heaven.' "
MATTHEW 6:9–10 NIV

JANUARY 2022

SUNDAY	MONDAY	TUESDAY	WEDNESDAY
26	27	28	29
2	3	4	5
9	10	11	12
16	17 _Martin Luther King Jr. Day_	18	19
23 / 30	24 / 31	25	26

notes

THURSDAY	FRIDAY	SATURDAY
30	31	1
		New Year's Day
6	7	8
13	14	15
20	21	22
27	28	29

....
....
....
....
....
....
....
....
....
....
....

DECEMBER

S	M	T	W	T	F	S
			1	2	3	4
5	6	7	8	9	10	11
12	13	14	15	16	17	18
19	20	21	22	23	24	25
26	27	28	29	30	31	

FEBRUARY

S	M	T	W	T	F	S
		1	2	3	4	5
6	7	8	9	10	11	12
13	14	15	16	17	18	19
20	21	22	23	24	25	26
27	28					

WORK

*May the Lord our God show us his approval and make
our efforts successful. Yes, make our efforts successful!*
PSALM 90:17 NLT

Success is a funny word. It can indicate doing whatever it takes to climb your way to the top. It can also mean recognizing your worth at work based on what *God* says about who you are and what you're supposed to do.

"Once you understand the *why* behind work, you'll be able to pursue your career with confidence, embrace change, and approach your job with a whole heart—one that is fully submitted to God and ready for what He's called you to do. That's what makes work worth doing," says Tom Heetderks in his book *Work Worth Doing*. He emphasizes the key verse of 1 Samuel 16:7: "The LORD does not look at the things people look at. People look at the outward appearance, but the LORD looks at the heart" (NIV).

Imagine God filling your heart and smiling as you work. It's possible every day!

DEAR HEAVENLY FATHER, THANK YOU FOR. . .

....

....

....

HERE'S WHAT'S HAPPENING IN MY LIFE. . .

....

....

....

I need. . .

Amen.
Thank You, Father,
for hearing my prayers.

GOALS *for this* MONTH

*My son, do not forget my teaching, but let your heart keep my
commandments, for length of days and years of life and peace they
will add to you. Let not steadfast love and faithfulness forsake you;
bind them around your neck; write them on the tablet of your heart.
So you will find favor and good success in the sight of God and man.*
PROVERBS 3:1–4 ESV

JANUARY 2022

S	M	T	W	T	F	S
						1
2	3	4	5	6	7	8
9	10	11	12	13	14	15
16	17	18	19	20	21	22
23	24	25	26	27	28	29
30	31					

Wise people seek to grow in the Lord and in every major sphere of life—including their work. After all, work is where we invest the bulk of our waking hours each week. The average person works nearly a hundred thousand hours in their lifetime. Want to be successful? Then learn from the best.

to-do list

- [ ]
- [ ]
- [ ]
- [ ]
- [ ]
- [ ]
- [ ]
- [ ]
- [ ]
- [ ]
- [ ]
- [ ]
- [ ]
- [ ]
- [ ]
- [ ]
- [ ]
- [ ]

SUNDAY, JANUARY 2

MONDAY, JANUARY 3

TUESDAY, JANUARY 4

WEDNESDAY, JANUARY 5

....
....
....
....
....

THURSDAY, JANUARY 6

....
....
....
....
....

FRIDAY, JANUARY 7

....
....
....
....
....

SATURDAY, JANUARY 8

....
....
....
....
....

to-do list

☐ ....
☐ ....
☐ ....
☐ ....
☐ ....
☐ ....
☐ ....
☐ ....
☐ ....
☐ ....
☐ ....
☐ ....
☐ ....
☐ ....
☐ ....
☐ ....

*Whatever you have
learned or received or
heard from me, or seen in
me—put it into practice.*
PHILIPPIANS 4:9 NIV

JANUARY 2022

S	M	T	W	T	F	S
						1
2	3	4	5	6	7	8
9	10	11	12	13	14	15
16	17	18	19	20	21	22
23	24	25	26	27	28	29
30	31					

Natural strengths are certain traits that God gave us. If we operate within these strengths, we thrive. But if we try to convert a personal weakness into a strength, then operate out of this "learned" strength, we'll generally fail. Why? Because it takes so much work to operate out of learned strengths, we either burn out or flee back to our natural strengths.

to-do list

- [ ] ....
- [ ] ....
- [ ] ....
- [ ] ....
- [ ] ....
- [ ] ....
- [ ] ....
- [ ] ....
- [ ] ....
- [ ] ....
- [ ] ....
- [ ] ....
- [ ] ....
- [ ] ....
- [ ] ....
- [ ] ....
- [ ] ....
- [ ] ....
- [ ] ....

SUNDAY, JANUARY 9

MONDAY, JANUARY 10

TUESDAY, JANUARY 11

WEDNESDAY, JANUARY 12

....
....
....
....
....

THURSDAY, JANUARY 13

....
....
....
....
....

FRIDAY, JANUARY 14

....
....
....
....
....

SATURDAY, JANUARY 15

....
....
....
....
....

to-do list

- ☐ ....
- ☐ ....
- ☐ ....
- ☐ ....
- ☐ ....
- ☐ ....
- ☐ ....
- ☐ ....
- ☐ ....
- ☐ ....
- ☐ ....
- ☐ ....
- ☐ ....
- ☐ ....
- ☐ ....
- ☐ ....

By the grace of God I am what I am, and his grace to me was not without effect. No, I worked harder than all of them—yet not I, but the grace of God that was with me.
1 CORINTHIANS 15:10 NIV

JANUARY 2022

S	M	T	W	T	F	S
						1
2	3	4	5	6	7	8
9	10	11	12	13	14	15
16	17	18	19	20	21	22
23	24	25	26	27	28	29
30	31					

Your boss may never ask you to work overseas—though he could. Or what if your boss offered you a leadership training program? Or some other challenge that stretched you? Would you be willing to say yes? If so, God may use you in ways you never dreamed possible.

to-do list

☐ ....
☐ ....
☐ ....
☐ ....
☐ ....
☐ ....
☐ ....
☐ ....
☐ ....
☐ ....
☐ ....
☐ ....
☐ ....
☐ ....
☐ ....
☐ ....
☐ ....
☐ ....
☐ ....

SUNDAY, JANUARY 16

MONDAY, JANUARY 17
Martin Luther King Jr. Day

TUESDAY, JANUARY 18

WEDNESDAY, JANUARY 19

THURSDAY, JANUARY 20

FRIDAY, JANUARY 21

SATURDAY, JANUARY 22

to-do list

☐
☐
☐
☐
☐
☐
☐
☐
☐
☐
☐
☐
☐
☐
☐
☐

Do you see someone skilled in their work? They will serve before kings; they will not serve before officials of low rank.
PROVERBS 22:29 NIV

JANUARY 2022

S	M	T	W	T	F	S
						1
2	3	4	5	6	7	8
9	10	11	12	13	14	15
16	17	18	19	20	21	22
23	24	25	26	27	28	29
30	31					

What do you predict about your own job? Will it look the same in a few years? Will it be there at all? Or should you be making shifts to your work mindset now? In other words, what limiting beliefs should you shed in order to successfully prepare for your future work?

to-do list

- [ ] ....
- [ ] ....
- [ ] ....
- [ ] ....
- [ ] ....
- [ ] ....
- [ ] ....
- [ ] ....
- [ ] ....
- [ ] ....
- [ ] ....
- [ ] ....
- [ ] ....
- [ ] ....
- [ ] ....
- [ ] ....
- [ ] ....
- [ ] ....

SUNDAY, JANUARY 23

....
....
....
....
....

MONDAY, JANUARY 24

....
....
....
....

TUESDAY, JANUARY 25

....
....
....
....
....

WEDNESDAY, JANUARY 26

THURSDAY, JANUARY 27

FRIDAY, JANUARY 28

SATURDAY, JANUARY 29

- [ ]
- [ ]
- [ ]
- [ ]
- [ ]
- [ ]
- [ ]
- [ ]
- [ ]
- [ ]
- [ ]
- [ ]
- [ ]
- [ ]
- [ ]
- [ ]

For God has not given us a spirit of fear and timidity, but of power, love, and self-discipline.
2 TIMOTHY 1:7 NLT

FEBRUARY 2022

SUNDAY	MONDAY	TUESDAY	WEDNESDAY
30	31	1	2
6	7	8	9
13	14 *Valentine's Day*	15	16
20	21 *Presidents' Day*	22	23
27	28	1	2

notes

THURSDAY	FRIDAY	SATURDAY
3	4	5
10	11	12
17	18	19
24	25	26
3	4	5

....
....
....
....
....
....
....
....
....
....
....
....
....

JANUARY

S	M	T	W	T	F	S
						1
2	3	4	5	6	7	8
9	10	11	12	13	14	15
16	17	18	19	20	21	22
23	24	25	26	27	28	29
30	31					

MARCH

S	M	T	W	T	F	S
		1	2	3	4	5
6	7	8	9	10	11	12
13	14	15	16	17	18	19
20	21	22	23	24	25	26
27	28	29	30	31		

MY *February* LIFE MAP

REST

You [the LORD] will keep in perfect peace those whose minds are steadfast, because they trust in you.
ISAIAH 26:3 NIV

The devil likes to twist God's good gifts—whether art and music, the act of sex, or even our Sabbath days. A Sabbath is dedicated to doing something different from other periods of time. In the Bible, the Sabbath meant a day without work each week—each Sabbath started early Friday evening and finished early Saturday evening. They were days of rest and worship and reflection.

A Sabbath rest is required by the Ten Commandments. But that's the only one of the Ten Commandments *not* repeated in the teachings of Jesus and His apostles. It's not that Sabbaths are obsolete, though. In our busy lives, they're more important than ever.

For many of us, Sunday is a good Sabbath day. But you can schedule one on another day of the week if your work schedule demands. Whatever day it is, prioritize rest and reflection. Include Bible reading, prayer, praise, and other forms of worship. You'll find that the exercise of the Sabbath brings rest.

DEAR HEAVENLY FATHER, THANK YOU FOR. . .

HERE'S WHAT'S HAPPENING IN MY LIFE. . .

OTHER THINGS ON MY HEART THAT
I NEED TO SHARE WITH YOU, GOD. . .

....

....

....

....

....

....

....

I need. . .

....

....

....

....

....

....

Amen.

Thank You, Father,
for hearing my prayers.

GOALS *for this* MONTH

....

....

....

....

....

....

....

....

*[Jesus said,] "Come to me, all you who are weary
and burdened, and I will give you rest."*
MATTHEW 11:28 NIV

FEBRUARY 2022

S	M	T	W	T	F	S
		1	2	3	4	5
6	7	8	9	10	11	12
13	14	15	16	17	18	19
20	21	22	23	24	25	26
27	28					

What do you do after work? Is there an "after work"? Ask God to help you rest.

to-do list

☐ ....
☐ ....
☐ ....
☐ ....
☐ ....
☐ ....
☐ ....
☐ ....
☐ ....
☐ ....
☐ ....
☐ ....
☐ ....
☐ ....
☐ ....
☐ ....
☐ ....
☐ ....
☐ ....

SUNDAY, JANUARY 30

MONDAY, JANUARY 31

TUESDAY, FEBRUARY 1

WEDNESDAY, FEBRUARY 2

THURSDAY, FEBRUARY 3

FRIDAY, FEBRUARY 4

SATURDAY, FEBRUARY 5

In vain you rise early and stay up late, toiling for food to eat—for [the LORD] grants sleep to those he loves.
PSALM 127:2 NIV

FEBRUARY 2022

S	M	T	W	T	F	S
		1	2	3	4	5
6	7	8	9	10	11	12
13	14	15	16	17	18	19
20	21	22	23	24	25	26
27	28					

Going to bed at the same time every night helps our sleep. And so does keeping the bedroom's temperature a few degrees cooler than normal. Turn off all screens at least an hour before retiring, and make sure the TV is in another room. God made the human body to need rest. Don't short-circuit that good night's sleep He offers.

to-do list

- [ ] ....
- [ ] ....
- [ ] ....
- [ ] ....
- [ ] ....
- [ ] ....
- [ ] ....
- [ ] ....
- [ ] ....
- [ ] ....
- [ ] ....
- [ ] ....
- [ ] ....
- [ ] ....
- [ ] ....
- [ ] ....
- [ ] ....
- [ ] ....

SUNDAY, FEBRUARY 6

MONDAY, FEBRUARY 7

TUESDAY, FEBRUARY 8

WEDNESDAY, FEBRUARY 9

THURSDAY, FEBRUARY 10

FRIDAY, FEBRUARY 11

SATURDAY, FEBRUARY 12

to-do list

- [ ]
- [ ]
- [ ]
- [ ]
- [ ]
- [ ]
- [ ]
- [ ]
- [ ]
- [ ]
- [ ]
- [ ]
- [ ]
- [ ]
- [ ]
- [ ]

*I lie down and sleep;
I wake again, because
the LORD sustains me.*
PSALM 3:5 NIV

FEBRUARY 2022

S	M	T	W	T	F	S
		1	2	3	4	5
6	7	8	9	10	11	12
13	14	15	16	17	18	19
20	21	22	23	24	25	26
27	28					

Before we take a power nap or drop off to sleep at night, our brains needle us with reminders of things we still need to do. For many of us, if we don't write each one down immediately, our brains just won't let us rest. Make a habit of taking notes throughout the day on a pad of sticky notes or with a note-to-self text message on your phone.

to-do list

☐ ....
☐ ....
☐ ....
☐ ....
☐ ....
☐ ....
☐ ....
☐ ....
☐ ....
☐ ....
☐ ....
☐ ....
☐ ....
☐ ....
☐ ....
☐ ....
☐ ....
☐ ....
☐ ....

SUNDAY, FEBRUARY 13

MONDAY, FEBRUARY 14   Valentine's Day

TUESDAY, FEBRUARY 15

WEDNESDAY, FEBRUARY 16

....
....
....
....
....

THURSDAY, FEBRUARY 17

....
....
....
....
....

FRIDAY, FEBRUARY 18

....
....
....
....
....

SATURDAY, FEBRUARY 19

....
....
....
....
....

to-do list

- [ ] ....
- [ ] ....
- [ ] ....
- [ ] ....
- [ ] ....
- [ ] ....
- [ ] ....
- [ ] ....
- [ ] ....
- [ ] ....
- [ ] ....
- [ ] ....
- [ ] ....
- [ ] ....
- [ ] ....
- [ ] ....

*At this I awoke and
looked around. My sleep
had been pleasant to me.*
JEREMIAH 31:26 NIV

FEBRUARY 2022

S	M	T	W	T	F	S
		1	2	3	4	5
6	7	8	9	10	11	12
13	14	15	16	17	18	19
20	21	22	23	24	25	26
27	28					

An old adage says, "Work as if it all depends on you. Pray as if it all depends on God." It's a pithy saying that has the ring of truth but sadly falls short. Bottom line: it all depends on *God*. If we do His will, we can leave the rest in His hands.

to-do list

- [ ] ....
- [ ] ....
- [ ] ....
- [ ] ....
- [ ] ....
- [ ] ....
- [ ] ....
- [ ] ....
- [ ] ....
- [ ] ....
- [ ] ....
- [ ] ....
- [ ] ....
- [ ] ....
- [ ] ....
- [ ] ....
- [ ] ....
- [ ] ....
- [ ] ....

SUNDAY, FEBRUARY 20

MONDAY, FEBRUARY 21 *Presidents' Day*

TUESDAY, FEBRUARY 22

WEDNESDAY, FEBRUARY 23

THURSDAY, FEBRUARY 24

FRIDAY, FEBRUARY 25

SATURDAY, FEBRUARY 26

to-do list

- [ ]
- [ ]
- [ ]
- [ ]
- [ ]
- [ ]
- [ ]
- [ ]
- [ ]
- [ ]
- [ ]
- [ ]
- [ ]
- [ ]
- [ ]
- [ ]

*"In returning and rest
you shall be saved;
in quietness and in trust
shall be your strength."*
ISAIAH 30:15 ESV

MARCH 2022

SUNDAY	MONDAY	TUESDAY	WEDNESDAY
27	28	1	2 *Ash Wednesday*
6	7	8	9
13 *Daylight Saving Time Begins*	14	15	16
20 *First Day of Spring*	21	22	23
27	28	29	30

notes

THURSDAY	FRIDAY	SATURDAY
3	4	5
10	11	12
17	18	19
St. Patrick's Day		
24	25	26
31	1	2

....
....
....
....
....
....
....
....
....
....
....
....
....
....
....
....

FEBRUARY

S	M	T	W	T	F	S
		1	2	3	4	5
6	7	8	9	10	11	12
13	14	15	16	17	18	19
20	21	22	23	24	25	26
27	28					

APRIL

S	M	T	W	T	F	S
					1	2
3	4	5	6	7	8	9
10	11	12	13	14	15	16
17	18	19	20	21	22	23
24	25	26	27	28	29	30

RECREATION

*There is a time for everything, and a season
for every activity under the heavens.*
ECCLESIASTES 3:1 NIV

God created humans to explore and discover and enjoy the world He made. But as finite beings, we can't just keep going. Just as we need rest, we also need restoration.

Recreational activities engage our minds and bodies in new ways, providing much-needed enjoyment. Recreation can happen anywhere, but getting outside in our very "inside" culture enables our minds and bodies to renew. Not surprisingly, practitioners of both physical and mental health recommend regularly spending time in nature.

This month let's look at recreation in a new way—not just as another activity but as a practice of refreshment. Let's explore how to recreate our minds, bodies, emotions, and spirits.

DEAR HEAVENLY FATHER, THANK YOU FOR. . .

HERE'S WHAT'S HAPPENING IN MY LIFE. . .

I need. . .

Amen.
Thank You, Father,
for hearing my prayers.

GOALS *for this* MONTH

"My purpose is to give them
a rich and satisfying life."
JOHN 10:10 NLT

MARCH 2022

S	M	T	W	T	F	S
		1	2	3	4	5
6	7	8	9	10	11	12
13	14	15	16	17	18	19
20	21	22	23	24	25	26
27	28	29	30	31		

Open your calendar today and schedule some days for recreation, even if you don't know what activities you'll do. If you don't set time aside for recreation, the days will fill up with other things. Planning ahead helps to ensure recreation happens.

to-do list

- ☐ ....
- ☐ ....
- ☐ ....
- ☐ ....
- ☐ ....
- ☐ ....
- ☐ ....
- ☐ ....
- ☐ ....
- ☐ ....
- ☐ ....
- ☐ ....
- ☐ ....
- ☐ ....
- ☐ ....
- ☐ ....
- ☐ ....
- ☐ ....

SUNDAY, FEBRUARY 27

MONDAY, FEBRUARY 28

TUESDAY, MARCH 1

WEDNESDAY, MARCH 2 *Ash Wednesday*

....
....
....
....
....

THURSDAY, MARCH 3

....
....
....
....
....

FRIDAY, MARCH 4

....
....
....
....
....

SATURDAY, MARCH 5

....
....
....
....
....

to-do list

- [ ] ....
- [ ] ....
- [ ] ....
- [ ] ....
- [ ] ....
- [ ] ....
- [ ] ....
- [ ] ....
- [ ] ....
- [ ] ....
- [ ] ....
- [ ] ....
- [ ] ....
- [ ] ....
- [ ] ....
- [ ] ....
- [ ] ....

The LORD has compassion on those who fear him; for he knows how we are formed, he remembers that we are dust.
PSALM 103:13–14 NIV

MARCH 2022

S	M	T	W	T	F	S
		1	2	3	4	5
6	7	8	9	10	11	12
13	14	15	16	17	18	19
20	21	22	23	24	25	26
27	28	29	30	31		

Not every activity refreshes your body, soul, and spirit. Trying new things enriches you, but doing what you *love* rejuvenates you. What are your recovery needs? Something that slows your mind and body—or something that gets your heart rate pumping? What about activities that allow you to lose track of time and let your creativity flow?

to-do list

- [ ] ....
- [ ] ....
- [ ] ....
- [ ] ....
- [ ] ....
- [ ] ....
- [ ] ....
- [ ] ....
- [ ] ....
- [ ] ....
- [ ] ....
- [ ] ....
- [ ] ....
- [ ] ....
- [ ] ....
- [ ] ....
- [ ] ....
- [ ] ....

SUNDAY, MARCH 6

MONDAY, MARCH 7

TUESDAY, MARCH 8

WEDNESDAY, MARCH 9

THURSDAY, MARCH 10

FRIDAY, MARCH 11

SATURDAY, MARCH 12

to-do list

☐
☐
☐
☐
☐
☐
☐
☐
☐
☐
☐
☐
☐
☐
☐
☐
☐

*[The LORD] satisfies your
desires with good things
so that your youth is
renewed like the eagle's.*
PSALM 103:5 NIV

MARCH 2022

S	M	T	W	T	F	S
		1	2	3	4	5
6	7	8	9	10	11	12
13	14	15	16	17	18	19
20	21	22	23	24	25	26
27	28	29	30	31		

Budget for and invest in recreation. You might join a local rec team or get a pass to the nearest public swimming pool, YMCA, or state or national park. If a particular activity becomes a favorite, its costs meet the real need of caring for yourself. Whatever you enjoy doing, remember that it is a gift of God. And when you enjoy it with thanksgiving, it can be a form of worship!

to-do list

- [ ] ....
- [ ] ....
- [ ] ....
- [ ] ....
- [ ] ....
- [ ] ....
- [ ] ....
- [ ] ....
- [ ] ....
- [ ] ....
- [ ] ....
- [ ] ....
- [ ] ....
- [ ] ....
- [ ] ....
- [ ] ....
- [ ] ....
- [ ] ....

SUNDAY, MARCH 13
Daylight Saving Time Begins

MONDAY, MARCH 14

TUESDAY, MARCH 15

WEDNESDAY, MARCH 16

THURSDAY, MARCH 17 *St. Patrick's Day*

FRIDAY, MARCH 18

SATURDAY, MARCH 19

to-do list

- [ ]
- [ ]
- [ ]
- [ ]
- [ ]
- [ ]
- [ ]
- [ ]
- [ ]
- [ ]
- [ ]
- [ ]
- [ ]
- [ ]
- [ ]
- [ ]

Whatever is good and perfect is a gift coming down to us from God our Father, who created all the lights in the heavens. He never changes or casts a shifting shadow.
JAMES 1:17 NLT

MARCH 2022

S	M	T	W	T	F	S
		1	2	3	4	5
6	7	8	9	10	11	12
13	14	15	16	17	18	19
20	21	22	23	24	25	26
27	28	29	30	31		

You can even ask your friends to include you in their recreational activities. When you're looking to improve your mental and emotional health, why not include the important people God has put in your life?

to-do list

☐ ....
☐ ....
☐ ....
☐ ....
☐ ....
☐ ....
☐ ....
☐ ....
☐ ....
☐ ....
☐ ....
☐ ....
☐ ....
☐ ....
☐ ....
☐ ....
☐ ....
☐ ....
☐ ....

SUNDAY, MARCH 20 *First Day of Spring*

MONDAY, MARCH 21

TUESDAY, MARCH 22

WEDNESDAY, MARCH 23

THURSDAY, MARCH 24

FRIDAY, MARCH 25

SATURDAY, MARCH 26

to-do list

- [ ]
- [ ]
- [ ]
- [ ]
- [ ]
- [ ]
- [ ]
- [ ]
- [ ]
- [ ]
- [ ]
- [ ]
- [ ]
- [ ]
- [ ]
- [ ]
- [ ]

[Jesus] said to them, "Come with me by yourselves to a quiet place and get some rest."
MARK 6:31 NIV

MARCH 2022

S	M	T	W	T	F	S
		1	2	3	4	5
6	7	8	9	10	11	12
13	14	15	16	17	18	19
20	21	22	23	24	25	26
27	28	29	30	31		

Do you have too many or too few outings on your calendar? Why not sit down today and plan something—or cancel an activity or two—so you can truly experience the joy and refreshment of recreation?

to-do list

- [ ]
- [ ]
- [ ]
- [ ]
- [ ]
- [ ]
- [ ]
- [ ]
- [ ]
- [ ]
- [ ]
- [ ]
- [ ]
- [ ]
- [ ]
- [ ]
- [ ]
- [ ]
- [ ]

SUNDAY, MARCH 27

MONDAY, MARCH 28

TUESDAY, MARCH 29

WEDNESDAY, MARCH 30

THURSDAY, MARCH 31

FRIDAY, APRIL 1

SATURDAY, APRIL 2

- [ ]
- [ ]
- [ ]
- [ ]
- [ ]
- [ ]
- [ ]
- [ ]
- [ ]
- [ ]
- [ ]
- [ ]
- [ ]
- [ ]
- [ ]

O Lord, what a variety of things you have made! In wisdom you have made them all.
PSALM 104:24 NLT

APRIL 2022

SUNDAY	MONDAY	TUESDAY	WEDNESDAY
27	28	29	30
3	4	5	6
10	11	12	13
Palm Sunday			
17	18	19	20
Easter			
24	25	26	27

notes

THURSDAY	FRIDAY	SATURDAY
31	1	2
7	8	9
14	15 *Good Friday / Passover Begins at Sundown*	16
21	22	23
28	29	30

....
....
....
....
....
....
....
....
....
....
....
....
....
....
....

MARCH

S	M	T	W	T	F	S
		1	2	3	4	5
6	7	8	9	10	11	12
13	14	15	16	17	18	19
20	21	22	23	24	25	26
27	28	29	30	31		

MAY

S	M	T	W	T	F	S
1	2	3	4	5	6	7
8	9	10	11	12	13	14
15	16	17	18	19	20	21
22	23	24	25	26	27	28
29	30	31				

ENTERTAINMENT

Finally, brothers and sisters, whatever is true, whatever is noble, whatever is right, whatever is pure, whatever is lovely, whatever is admirable— if anything is excellent or praiseworthy—think about such things.
PHILIPPIANS 4:8 NIV

"The big picture" doesn't necessarily mean the latest blockbuster movie. For Christians, it is the very important principle of Philippians 4:8.

The apostle Paul's words encapsulate and elaborate other teachings throughout scripture. Paul also wrote Romans 8:6 ("The mind governed by the flesh is death, but the mind governed by the Spirit is life and peace"; NIV), Ephesians 4:17 ("I tell you this, and insist on it in the Lord, that you must no longer live as the Gentiles do, in the futility of their thinking"; NIV), and 1 Corinthians 2:16 ("We have the mind of Christ"; NIV). And the Psalms and Proverbs contain many instructions on how to be wise and godly in our thoughts (for example, Psalms 1:2; 63:6; 77:12; 119:15; 143:5).

The point is simply this: God wants us to engage our minds with Him and His truth. Some forms of entertainment will help us to do that. Others will be neutral, and some will actively oppose the Lord. Let's approach our entertainment wisely.

DEAR HEAVENLY FATHER, THANK YOU FOR. . .

HERE'S WHAT'S HAPPENING IN MY LIFE. . .

I need. . .

....
....
....
....
....
....
....

OTHER THINGS ON MY HEART THAT I NEED TO SHARE WITH YOU, GOD. . .

....
....
....
....
....
....
....

Amen.
Thank You, Father,
for hearing my prayers.

GOALS *for this* MONTH

....
....
....
....
....
....
....
....

*Whether you eat or drink or whatever you do,
do it all for the glory of God.*
1 CORINTHIANS 10:31 NIV

APRIL 2022

S	M	T	W	T	F	S
					1	2
3	4	5	6	7	8	9
10	11	12	13	14	15	16
17	18	19	20	21	22	23
24	25	26	27	28	29	30

In our culture, entertainment is everywhere. It's almost impossible to avoid celebrities, athletes, and their work. A lot of entertainment is great, either as a way to relax or be challenged to see the world through new eyes. Some aspects of our entertainment culture, though, require some real discernment.

to-do list

- [ ]
- [ ]
- [ ]
- [ ]
- [ ]
- [ ]
- [ ]
- [ ]
- [ ]
- [ ]
- [ ]
- [ ]
- [ ]
- [ ]
- [ ]
- [ ]
- [ ]
- [ ]
- [ ]

SUNDAY, APRIL 3

MONDAY, APRIL 4

TUESDAY, APRIL 5

WEDNESDAY, APRIL 6

THURSDAY, APRIL 7

FRIDAY, APRIL 8

SATURDAY, APRIL 9

- [ ]
- [ ]
- [ ]
- [ ]
- [ ]
- [ ]
- [ ]
- [ ]
- [ ]
- [ ]
- [ ]
- [ ]
- [ ]
- [ ]
- [ ]
- [ ]

Guard your heart above all else, for it determines the course of your life.
PROVERBS 4:23 NLT

APRIL 2022

S	M	T	W	T	F	S
					1	2
3	4	5	6	7	8	9
10	11	12	13	14	15	16
17	18	19	20	21	22	23
24	25	26	27	28	29	30

The apostle Paul was very aware of the entertainment culture of his day, referencing poets, plays, and sporting events. Always, he used these examples to make distinctly Christian points. As you approach entertainment options, why not do the same thing? Watch, listen, and experience with a goal of seeing Jesus more clearly.

to-do list

- [ ]
- [ ]
- [ ]
- [ ]
- [ ]
- [ ]
- [ ]
- [ ]
- [ ]
- [ ]
- [ ]
- [ ]
- [ ]
- [ ]
- [ ]
- [ ]
- [ ]
- [ ]
- [ ]

SUNDAY, APRIL 10 *Palm Sunday*

MONDAY, APRIL 11

TUESDAY, APRIL 12

WEDNESDAY, APRIL 13

THURSDAY, APRIL 14

FRIDAY, APRIL 15

*Good Friday
Passover Begins
at Sundown*

SATURDAY, APRIL 16

to-do list

☐
☐
☐
☐
☐
☐
☐
☐
☐
☐
☐
☐
☐
☐
☐
☐

"As some of your
own poets have said,
'We are his offspring.' "
ACTS 17:28 NIV

APRIL 2022

S	M	T	W	T	F	S
					1	2
3	4	5	6	7	8	9
10	11	12	13	14	15	16
17	18	19	20	21	22	23
24	25	26	27	28	29	30

We often turn to entertainment to escape, to get away from the troubles and frustrations of real life. There's a lot of value in that, but as Christians we help ourselves by keeping our brains (and spirits) engaged.

to-do list

- [ ] ....
- [ ] ....
- [ ] ....
- [ ] ....
- [ ] ....
- [ ] ....
- [ ] ....
- [ ] ....
- [ ] ....
- [ ] ....
- [ ] ....
- [ ] ....
- [ ] ....
- [ ] ....
- [ ] ....
- [ ] ....
- [ ] ....
- [ ] ....

SUNDAY, APRIL 17 — *Easter*

MONDAY, APRIL 18

TUESDAY, APRIL 19

WEDNESDAY, APRIL 20

....

....

....

....

....

THURSDAY, APRIL 21

....

....

....

....

FRIDAY, APRIL 22

....

....

....

....

....

SATURDAY, APRIL 23

....

....

....

....

....

to-do list

☐ ....
☐ ....
☐ ....
☐ ....
☐ ....
☐ ....
☐ ....
☐ ....
☐ ....
☐ ....
☐ ....
☐ ....
☐ ....
☐ ....
☐ ....
☐ ....
☐ ....

We use our powerful God-tools for smashing warped philosophies, tearing down barriers erected against the truth of God, fitting every loose thought and emotion and impulse into the structure of life shaped by Christ.
2 CORINTHIANS 10:5 MSG

APRIL 2022

S	M	T	W	T	F	S
					1	2
3	4	5	6	7	8	9
10	11	12	13	14	15	16
17	18	19	20	21	22	23
24	25	26	27	28	29	30

Allow your entertainment choices to generate gratitude to God—either for their positive, uplifting messages or for the realization of what He has saved you from.

to-do list

- [ ]
- [ ]
- [ ]
- [ ]
- [ ]
- [ ]
- [ ]
- [ ]
- [ ]
- [ ]
- [ ]
- [ ]
- [ ]
- [ ]
- [ ]
- [ ]
- [ ]
- [ ]

SUNDAY, APRIL 24

MONDAY, APRIL 25

TUESDAY, APRIL 26

WEDNESDAY, APRIL 27

....
....
....
....
....

THURSDAY, APRIL 28

....
....
....
....
....

FRIDAY, APRIL 29

....
....
....
....
....

SATURDAY, APRIL 30

....
....
....
....
....

to-do list

- [ ]
- [ ]
- [ ]
- [ ]
- [ ]
- [ ]
- [ ]
- [ ]
- [ ]
- [ ]
- [ ]
- [ ]
- [ ]
- [ ]
- [ ]
- [ ]

Discretion will protect you, and understanding will guard you.
PROVERBS 2:11 NIV

MAY 2022

SUNDAY	MONDAY	TUESDAY	WEDNESDAY
1	2	3	4
8 *Mother's Day*	9	10	11
15	16	17	18
22	23	24	25
29	30 *Memorial Day*	31	1

notes

THURSDAY	FRIDAY	SATURDAY
5	6	7
National Day of Prayer		
12	13	14
19	20	21
26	27	28
2	3	4

....
....
....
....
....
....
....
....
....
....
....
....
....
....
....

APRIL

S	M	T	W	T	F	S
					1	2
3	4	5	6	7	8	9
10	11	12	13	14	15	16
17	18	19	20	21	22	23
24	25	26	27	28	29	30

JUNE

S	M	T	W	T	F	S
			1	2	3	4
5	6	7	8	9	10	11
12	13	14	15	16	17	18
19	20	21	22	23	24	25
26	27	28	29	30		

PERSONAL IMPROVEMENT

It is God who works in you to will and
to act in order to fulfill his good purpose.
PHILIPPIANS 2:13 NIV

If there is any area of life where we need to depend on the Lord fully and completely, it's the area of growing *volitionally*. What does that mean? We all make choices hundreds of times a day. God doesn't really care about the color of your socks. But He cares deeply about your choices for and against His written Word, the Bible. What's more, He cares deeply about your decisions for and against your "neighbors"—including your family and friends and colleagues.

Beverage companies make it seem like a big deal, but what you drink with lunch won't register on the Richter scale. What you think about another person at lunch, or what you say to her, or *how* you say it—now, those are the kinds of choices God watches.

Here are three ways to grow volitionally: (1) Don't sweat life's little decisions. (2) Do sweat how you impact others. (3) When you blow it, apologize.

DEAR HEAVENLY FATHER, THANK YOU FOR. . .

HERE'S WHAT'S HAPPENING IN MY LIFE. . .

OTHER THINGS ON MY HEART THAT
I NEED TO SHARE WITH YOU, GOD. . .

....
....
....
....
....
....

I need. . .

....
....
....
....
....
....
....
....

Amen.
Thank You, Father,
for hearing my prayers.

GOALS *for this* MONTH

....
....
....
....
....
....
....
....

I press on toward the goal to win the prize for
which God has called me heavenward in Christ Jesus.
PHILIPPIANS 3:14 NIV

MAY 2022

S	M	T	W	T	F	S
	2	3	4	5	6	7
8	9	10	11	12	13	14
15	16	17	18	19	20	21
22	23	24	25	26	27	28
29	30	31				

In the garden of our soul, God's first job is to trim back the branches and twigs. How we choose to experience that trimming is so important: Are we mourning our losses or anticipating growth? After that, how do we choose to experience the wind, rain, hail, clouds, and sunshine He sends? Do we see them all as God's good hand of blessing for our spiritual fruitfulness?

to-do list

- [ ]
- [ ]
- [ ]
- [ ]
- [ ]
- [ ]
- [ ]
- [ ]
- [ ]
- [ ]
- [ ]
- [ ]
- [ ]
- [ ]
- [ ]
- [ ]
- [ ]
- [ ]
- [ ]

SUNDAY, MAY 1

MONDAY, MAY 2

TUESDAY, MAY 3

WEDNESDAY, MAY 4

THURSDAY, MAY 5
National Day of Prayer

FRIDAY, MAY 6

SATURDAY, MAY 7

to-do list

☐
☐
☐
☐
☐
☐
☐
☐
☐
☐
☐
☐
☐
☐
☐
☐
☐

So neither the one who plants nor the one who waters is anything, but only God, who makes things grow.
1 CORINTHIANS 3:7 NIV

MAY 2022

S	M	T	W	T	F	S
1	2	3	4	5	6	7
8	9	10	11	12	13	14
15	16	17	18	19	20	21
22	23	24	25	26	27	28
29	30	31				

Here's an idea for deepening your relationships: purchase a pack of index cards and use them to jot down prayer needs of specific family members and friends. Make a commitment to pray for all of them weekly. Then start casually mentioning, "I pray for you every week." Then ask, "How can I best pray for you these next couple of weeks?"

to-do list

- [ ]
- [ ]
- [ ]
- [ ]
- [ ]
- [ ]
- [ ]
- [ ]
- [ ]
- [ ]
- [ ]
- [ ]
- [ ]
- [ ]
- [ ]
- [ ]
- [ ]
- [ ]
- [ ]

SUNDAY, MAY 8 — *Mother's Day*

MONDAY, MAY 9

TUESDAY, MAY 10

WEDNESDAY, MAY 11

THURSDAY, MAY 12

FRIDAY, MAY 13

SATURDAY, MAY 14

to-do list

☐
☐
☐
☐
☐
☐
☐
☐
☐
☐
☐
☐
☐
☐
☐
☐

We ought always to give thanks to God for you, brothers, as is right, because your faith is growing abundantly, and the love of every one of you for one another is increasing.
2 THESSALONIANS 1:3 ESV

MAY 2022

S	M	T	W	T	F	S
1	2	3	4	5	6	7
8	9	10	11	12	13	14
15	16	17	18	19	20	21
22	23	24	25	26	27	28
29	30	31				

Long gone are the days where every home had a family Bible. Yet reading God's Word, the Holy Scriptures, is what generates fear of the Lord and true wisdom (Job 28:28; Psalm 111:10; Proverbs 1:7; 2:5; 9:10; Ecclesiastes 12:12–14). Read other good books, certainly. But never neglect the Book of books!

to-do list

- [ ]
- [ ]
- [ ]
- [ ]
- [ ]
- [ ]
- [ ]
- [ ]
- [ ]
- [ ]
- [ ]
- [ ]
- [ ]
- [ ]
- [ ]
- [ ]
- [ ]
- [ ]
- [ ]

SUNDAY, MAY 15

MONDAY, MAY 16

TUESDAY, MAY 17

WEDNESDAY, MAY 18

THURSDAY, MAY 19

FRIDAY, MAY 20

SATURDAY, MAY 21

to-do list

- [ ]
- [ ]
- [ ]
- [ ]
- [ ]
- [ ]
- [ ]
- [ ]
- [ ]
- [ ]
- [ ]
- [ ]
- [ ]
- [ ]
- [ ]
- [ ]

Live a life worthy of the Lord and please him in every way: bearing fruit in every good work, growing in the knowledge of God.
COLOSSIANS 1:10 NIV

MAY 2022

S	M	T	W	T	F	S
1	2	3	4	5	6	7
8	9	10	11	12	13	14
15	16	17	18	19	20	21
22	23	24	25	26	27	28
29	30	31				

Often we wish personal improvement was like putting Miracle-Gro on the plants in a well-kept garden. "Just add prayer and Bible reading!"—and then spiritual, mental, and emotional growth appear. It doesn't work that way, though. Human beings need a long time to mature.

to-do list

☐ ....
☐ ....
☐ ....
☐ ....
☐ ....
☐ ....
☐ ....
☐ ....
☐ ....
☐ ....
☐ ....
☐ ....
☐ ....
☐ ....
☐ ....
☐ ....
☐ ....
☐ ....
☐ ....

SUNDAY, MAY 22

MONDAY, MAY 23

TUESDAY, MAY 24

WEDNESDAY, MAY 25

....
....
....
....
....

THURSDAY, MAY 26

....
....
....
....
....

FRIDAY, MAY 27

....
....
....
....
....

SATURDAY, MAY 28

....
....
....
....
....

to-do list

- [ ] ....
- [ ] ....
- [ ] ....
- [ ] ....
- [ ] ....
- [ ] ....
- [ ] ....
- [ ] ....
- [ ] ....
- [ ] ....
- [ ] ....
- [ ] ....
- [ ] ....
- [ ] ....
- [ ] ....
- [ ] ....

His delight is in the law of the LORD, and on his law he meditates day and night. He is like a tree planted by streams of water that yields its fruit in its season, and its leaf does not wither. In all that he does, he prospers.
PSALM 1:2–3 ESV

JUNE 2022

SUNDAY	MONDAY	TUESDAY	WEDNESDAY
29	30	31	1
5	6	7	8
12	13	14 *Flag Day*	15
19 *Father's Day*	20	21 *First Day of Summer*	22
26	27	28	29

notes

THURSDAY	FRIDAY	SATURDAY
2	3	4
9	10	11
16	17	18
23	24	25
30	1	2

....
....
....
....
....
....
....
....
....
....
....
....
....

MAY

S	M	T	W	T	F	S
1	2	3	4	5	6	7
8	9	10	11	12	13	14
15	16	17	18	19	20	21
22	23	24	25	26	27	28
29	30	31				

JULY

S	M	T	W	T	F	S
					1	2
3	4	5	6	7	8	9
10	11	12	13	14	15	16
17	18	19	20	21	22	23
24	25	26	27	28	29	30
31						

HEALTH AND FITNESS

*Everyone who competes in the games goes into strict
training. They do it to get a crown that will not last,
but we do it to get a crown that will last forever.*
1 CORINTHIANS 9:25 NIV

Throughout history, exercise happened primarily through the vigor of daily living: hauling water, chopping wood, tending gardens, washing clothes, making things. The Greeks had the luxury to put on competitions to demonstrate athletic prowess, but then, like now, few people are Olympians.

Today we know more than ever about the complex design of the human body—and how to care for it. For some people, exercise is about being as strong and fit as possible. For others, it means using specific exercises to address physical pain or challenges.

Find ways to take care of your own body. God has given you just one—so make it last!

DEAR HEAVENLY FATHER, THANK YOU FOR. . .

HERE'S WHAT'S HAPPENING IN MY LIFE. . .

OTHER THINGS ON MY HEART THAT I NEED TO SHARE WITH YOU, GOD. . .

I need. . .

Amen.
Thank You, Father,
for hearing my prayers.

GOALS *for this* MONTH

*Physical training is of some value, but godliness
has value for all things, holding promise for
both the present life and the life to come.*
1 TIMOTHY 4:8 NIV

JUNE 2022

S	M	T	W	T	F	S
			1	2	3	4
5	6	7	8	9	10	11
12	13	14	15	16	17	18
19	20	21	22	23	24	25
26	27	28	29	30		

Fitness doesn't require dangerous activity and lots of adrenaline. Surprisingly, the core of fitness comes down to a few basics, including good hydration, a healthy diet, intentional breaks, brisk walking, and selective exercises. Gratefully caring for the body God has given you is a form of worship.

to-do list

- ☐
- ☐
- ☐
- ☐
- ☐
- ☐
- ☐
- ☐
- ☐
- ☐
- ☐
- ☐
- ☐
- ☐
- ☐
- ☐
- ☐
- ☐
- ☐

SUNDAY, MAY 29

MONDAY, MAY 30 *Memorial Day*

TUESDAY, MAY 31

WEDNESDAY, JUNE 1

THURSDAY, JUNE 2

FRIDAY, JUNE 3

SATURDAY, JUNE 4

to-do list

- [ ]
- [ ]
- [ ]
- [ ]
- [ ]
- [ ]
- [ ]
- [ ]
- [ ]
- [ ]
- [ ]
- [ ]
- [ ]
- [ ]
- [ ]
- [ ]

*No one ever hated their
own body, but they feed
and care for their body, just
as Christ does the church.*
EPHESIANS 5:29 NIV

JUNE 2022

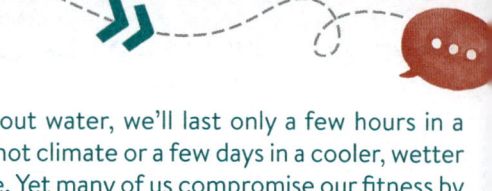

S	M	T	W	T	F	S
			1	2	3	4
5	6	7	8	9	10	11
12	13	14	15	16	17	18
19	20	21	22	23	24	25
26	27	28	29	30		

Without water, we'll last only a few hours in a dry, hot climate or a few days in a cooler, wetter place. Yet many of us compromise our fitness by failing to drink enough. When Jesus promised "living water" (John 4:10), He was describing a spiritual blessing. But isn't it instructive that He used *water* as His example?

to-do list

- [ ]
- [ ]
- [ ]
- [ ]
- [ ]
- [ ]
- [ ]
- [ ]
- [ ]
- [ ]
- [ ]
- [ ]
- [ ]
- [ ]
- [ ]
- [ ]
- [ ]
- [ ]
- [ ]

SUNDAY, JUNE 5

MONDAY, JUNE 6

TUESDAY, JUNE 7

WEDNESDAY, JUNE 8

....
....
....
....
....

THURSDAY, JUNE 9

....
....
....
....
....

FRIDAY, JUNE 10

....
....
....
....
....

SATURDAY, JUNE 11

....
....
....
....
....

to-do list

- [ ] ....
- [ ] ....
- [ ] ....
- [ ] ....
- [ ] ....
- [ ] ....
- [ ] ....
- [ ] ....
- [ ] ....
- [ ] ....
- [ ] ....
- [ ] ....
- [ ] ....
- [ ] ....
- [ ] ....
- [ ] ....

[Jesus said,] "If anyone gives even a cup of cold water to one of these little ones who is my disciple, truly I tell you, that person will certainly not lose their reward."
MATTHEW 10:42 NIV

JUNE 2022

S	M	T	W	T	F	S
			1	2	3	4
5	6	7	8	9	10	11
12	13	14	15	16	17	18
19	20	21	22	23	24	25
26	27	28	29	30		

One key to healthy eating? Receive whatever you eat *with thanksgiving.*

to-do list

- [ ] ....
- [ ] ....
- [ ] ....
- [ ] ....
- [ ] ....
- [ ] ....
- [ ] ....
- [ ] ....
- [ ] ....
- [ ] ....
- [ ] ....
- [ ] ....
- [ ] ....
- [ ] ....
- [ ] ....
- [ ] ....
- [ ] ....
- [ ] ....

SUNDAY, JUNE 12

MONDAY, JUNE 13

TUESDAY, JUNE 14   *Flag Day*

WEDNESDAY, JUNE 15

THURSDAY, JUNE 16

FRIDAY, JUNE 17

SATURDAY, JUNE 18

to-do list

- [ ]
- [ ]
- [ ]
- [ ]
- [ ]
- [ ]
- [ ]
- [ ]
- [ ]
- [ ]
- [ ]
- [ ]
- [ ]
- [ ]
- [ ]

For everything God created is good, and nothing is to be rejected if it is received with thanksgiving, because it is consecrated by the word of God and prayer.
1 TIMOTHY 4:4–5 NIV

JUNE 2022

S	M	T	W	T	F	S
			1	2	3	4
5	6	7	8	9	10	11
12	13	14	15	16	17	18
19	20	21	22	23	24	25
26	27	28	29	30		

In Bible times, people took intentional breaks. Sometimes the break was an evening nap in a boat (Mark 4:38). Sometimes it was an outdoor nap after eating (1 Kings 19:6). Sometimes it meant sitting in the shade in the heat of the day (Genesis 18:1). Thanks to the examples of Jesus, Elijah, and Abraham, we're encouraged to take breaks too—each in our own way.

to-do list

- ☐ ....
- ☐ ....
- ☐ ....
- ☐ ....
- ☐ ....
- ☐ ....
- ☐ ....
- ☐ ....
- ☐ ....
- ☐ ....
- ☐ ....
- ☐ ....
- ☐ ....
- ☐ ....
- ☐ ....
- ☐ ....
- ☐ ....
- ☐ ....

SUNDAY, JUNE 19   *Father's Day*

MONDAY, JUNE 20

TUESDAY, JUNE 21   *First Day of Summer*

WEDNESDAY, JUNE 22

....
....
....
....
....

THURSDAY, JUNE 23

....
....
....
....
....

FRIDAY, JUNE 24

....
....
....
....

SATURDAY, JUNE 25

....
....
....
....
....

to-do list

- [ ] ....
- [ ] ....
- [ ] ....
- [ ] ....
- [ ] ....
- [ ] ....
- [ ] ....
- [ ] ....
- [ ] ....
- [ ] ....
- [ ] ....
- [ ] ....
- [ ] ....
- [ ] ....
- [ ] ....
- [ ] ....

"[Ruth] said, 'Please let me glean and gather among the sheaves behind the harvesters.' She came into the field and has remained here from morning till now, except for a short rest in the shelter."
RUTH 2:7 NIV

JUNE 2022

S	M	T	W	T	F	S
			1	2	3	4
5	6	7	8	9	10	11
12	13	14	15	16	17	18
19	20	21	22	23	24	25
26	27	28	29	30		

God's Word often talks about walking. During three years of public ministry, Jesus walked through the territory of every tribe of Israel except one. Like Him, we can enjoy walking—and do it often. You'll find physical benefits but also refreshment for your mind and soul.

to-do list

- [ ] ....
- [ ] ....
- [ ] ....
- [ ] ....
- [ ] ....
- [ ] ....
- [ ] ....
- [ ] ....
- [ ] ....
- [ ] ....
- [ ] ....
- [ ] ....
- [ ] ....
- [ ] ....
- [ ] ....
- [ ] ....
- [ ] ....
- [ ] ....
- [ ] ....

SUNDAY, JUNE 26

MONDAY, JUNE 27

TUESDAY, JUNE 28

WEDNESDAY, JUNE 29

....
....
....
....
....

THURSDAY, JUNE 30

....
....
....
....
....

FRIDAY, JULY 1

....
....
....
....
....

SATURDAY, JULY 2

....
....
....
....
....

to-do list

- [ ] ....
- [ ] ....
- [ ] ....
- [ ] ....
- [ ] ....
- [ ] ....
- [ ] ....
- [ ] ....
- [ ] ....
- [ ] ....
- [ ] ....
- [ ] ....
- [ ] ....
- [ ] ....
- [ ] ....
- [ ] ....
- [ ] ....

"These words that I command you today shall be on your heart. You shall teach them diligently to your children, and shall talk of them when you sit in your house, and when you walk by the way."
DEUTERONOMY 6:6–7 ESV

JULY 2022

SUNDAY	MONDAY	TUESDAY	WEDNESDAY
26	27	28	29
3	4 *Independence Day*	5	6
10	11	12	13
17	18	19	20
24 31	25	26	27

notes

THURSDAY	FRIDAY	SATURDAY
30	1	2
7	8	9
14	15	16
21	22	23
28	29	30

JUNE

S	M	T	W	T	F	S
			1	2	3	4
5	6	7	8	9	10	11
12	13	14	15	16	17	18
19	20	21	22	23	24	25
26	27	28	29	30		

AUGUST

S	M	T	W	T	F	S
	1	2	3	4	5	6
7	8	9	10	11	12	13
14	15	16	17	18	19	20
21	22	23	24	25	26	27
28	29	30	31			

TRAVEL

He makes me lie down in green pastures, he leads me beside quiet waters, he refreshes my soul. He guides me along the right paths for his name's sake.
PSALM 23:2–3 NIV

Some people visit all the national parks, and others drive to Grandma's once a year. Some long for tropical paradises; others can't wait to visit historical sites. Some travel out of curiosity, to make connections, or simply to celebrate life.

If you step outside your state, you can experience your great country. If you step outside your country, you can get a bigger taste of this amazing planet. The most important step is to go!

Is there somewhere you've always wanted to go? Dust off that dream today. Why not begin planning a trip for the coming year? Revisit your travel dreams periodically, with the goal of actually going.

DEAR HEAVENLY FATHER, THANK YOU FOR. . .

....

....

....

HERE'S WHAT'S HAPPENING IN MY LIFE. . .

....

....

....

OTHER THINGS ON MY HEART THAT
I NEED TO SHARE WITH YOU, GOD. . .

I need. . .

Amen.
Thank You, Father,
for hearing my prayers.

GOALS *for this* MONTH

*The LORD will watch over your coming
and going both now and forevermore.*
PSALM 121:8 NIV

JULY 2022

S	M	T	W	T	F	S
					1	2
3	4	5	6	7	8	9
10	11	12	13	14	15	16
17	18	19	20	21	22	23
24	25	26	27	28	29	30
31						

Remember, travel isn't only a flight or cruise to an exotic location. Road trips offer many joys of their own. And railroad tracks often provide stunning views of the countryside.

to-do list

- ☐ ....
- ☐ ....
- ☐ ....
- ☐ ....
- ☐ ....
- ☐ ....
- ☐ ....
- ☐ ....
- ☐ ....
- ☐ ....
- ☐ ....
- ☐ ....
- ☐ ....
- ☐ ....
- ☐ ....
- ☐ ....
- ☐ ....
- ☐ ....
- ☐ ....

SUNDAY, JULY 3

MONDAY, JULY 4   *Independence Day*

TUESDAY, JULY 5

WEDNESDAY, JULY 6

THURSDAY, JULY 7

FRIDAY, JULY 8

SATURDAY, JULY 9

to-do list

- [ ]
- [ ]
- [ ]
- [ ]
- [ ]
- [ ]
- [ ]
- [ ]
- [ ]
- [ ]
- [ ]
- [ ]
- [ ]
- [ ]
- [ ]
- [ ]

"The LORD himself goes before you and will be with you; he will never leave you nor forsake you. Do not be afraid."
DEUTERONOMY 31:8 NIV

JULY 2022

S	M	T	W	T	F	S
					1	2
3	4	5	6	7	8	9
10	11	12	13	14	15	16
17	18	19	20	21	22	23
24	25	26	27	28	29	30
31						

Wherever you go, find something to appreciate, even if it's less than you expected. A tiny hotel room in Paris may not provide the best night's sleep, but you're there to have new experiences—not replicate home. Wherever you go, remember that God is with you—cheering you on!

to-do list

- [ ]
- [ ]
- [ ]
- [ ]
- [ ]
- [ ]
- [ ]
- [ ]
- [ ]
- [ ]
- [ ]
- [ ]
- [ ]
- [ ]
- [ ]
- [ ]
- [ ]
- [ ]
- [ ]

SUNDAY, JULY 10

MONDAY, JULY 11

TUESDAY, JULY 12

WEDNESDAY, JULY 13

to-do list

☐ ....
☐ ....
☐ ....
☐ ....
☐ ....
☐ ....
☐ ....
☐ ....
☐ ....
☐ ....
☐ ....
☐ ....
☐ ....
☐ ....
☐ ....
☐ ....
☐ ....

THURSDAY, JULY 14

FRIDAY, JULY 15

SATURDAY, JULY 16

The LORD makes firm the steps of the one who delights in him.
PSALM 37:23 NIV

JULY 2022

S	M	T	W	T	F	S
					1	2
3	4	5	6	7	8	9
10	11	12	13	14	15	16
17	18	19	20	21	22	23
24	25	26	27	28	29	30
31						

If you plan ahead, you can travel more often than you might guess. Why not start a travel savings account? If you use direct deposit from your paycheck, designate perhaps a few dollars for this account. After a few months, consider increasing that amount.

to-do list

- [ ]
- [ ]
- [ ]
- [ ]
- [ ]
- [ ]
- [ ]
- [ ]
- [ ]
- [ ]
- [ ]
- [ ]
- [ ]
- [ ]
- [ ]
- [ ]
- [ ]
- [ ]

SUNDAY, JULY 17

MONDAY, JULY 18

TUESDAY, JULY 19

WEDNESDAY, JULY 20

THURSDAY, JULY 21

FRIDAY, JULY 22

SATURDAY, JULY 23

to-do list

- [ ]
- [ ]
- [ ]
- [ ]
- [ ]
- [ ]
- [ ]
- [ ]
- [ ]
- [ ]
- [ ]
- [ ]
- [ ]
- [ ]
- [ ]
- [ ]

If I rise on the wings of the dawn, if I settle on the far side of the sea, even there your hand will guide me, your right hand will hold me fast.
PSALM 139:9–10 NIV

JULY 2022

S	M	T	W	T	F	S
					1	2
3	4	5	6	7	8	9
10	11	12	13	14	15	16
17	18	19	20	21	22	23
24	25	26	27	28	29	30
31						

Travel takes you away from your everyday responsibilities and transports you somewhere new. Whether your trip is exciting, educational, or restful, it promises more than just a good time. Travel expands your perspectives about other people. Best of all, you might return home with a bigger sense of God's heart for the world.

to-do list

☐
☐
☐
☐
☐
☐
☐
☐
☐
☐
☐
☐
☐
☐
☐
☐
☐
☐
☐

SUNDAY, JULY 24

MONDAY, JULY 25

TUESDAY, JULY 26

WEDNESDAY, JULY 27

THURSDAY, JULY 28

FRIDAY, JULY 29

SATURDAY, JULY 30

to-do list

- ☐
- ☐
- ☐
- ☐
- ☐
- ☐
- ☐
- ☐
- ☐
- ☐
- ☐
- ☐
- ☐
- ☐
- ☐
- ☐

I will instruct you and teach you in the way you should go; I will counsel you with my loving eye on you.
PSALM 32:8 NIV

AUGUST 2022

SUNDAY	MONDAY	TUESDAY	WEDNESDAY
31	1	2	3
7	8	9	10
14	15	16	17
21	22	23	24
28	29	30	31

notes

THURSDAY	FRIDAY	SATURDAY
4	5	6
11	12	13
18	19	20
25	26	27
1	2	3

....
....
....
....
....
....
....
....
....
....
....
....
....

JULY

S	M	T	W	T	F	S
					1	2
3	4	5	6	7	8	9
10	11	12	13	14	15	16
17	18	19	20	21	22	23
24	25	26	27	28	29	30
31						

SEPTEMBER

S	M	T	W	T	F	S
				1	2	3
4	5	6	7	8	9	10
11	12	13	14	15	16	17
18	19	20	21	22	23	24
25	26	27	28	29	30	

FINANCES

I know what it is to be in need, and I know what it is to have plenty.
I have learned the secret of being content in any and every situation,
whether well fed or hungry, whether living in plenty or in want.
PHILIPPIANS 4:12 NIV

The apostle Paul wrote, "I have learned to be content whatever the circumstances" (Philippians 4:11 NIV). Don't miss that word *learned*.

As a younger man, a member of the Pharisees, Paul (then known as Saul) was probably wealthy—likely a man who loved money (see Luke 16:14). As an apostle, however, he repeatedly lost his possessions to theft, riots, imprisonment, and shipwreck. As a result, he had known thirst and hunger, often going without food. Paul had even been cold and naked at times (see 2 Corinthians 11:23–27). He consistently worked hard to provide for his own needs and the needs of others (see Acts 18:3; Ephesians 4:28; 1 Thessalonians 4:11–12; 2 Thessalonians 3:6–15). Philippians 4:11 is not theory. Paul lived it out for decades—and we can too.

It's clear that Paul wasn't against wealth—he also wrote Philippians 4:12 above!

Perhaps the greatest gift any Christian could receive is this conviction: that "godliness with contentment is great gain" (1 Timothy 6:6).

DEAR HEAVENLY FATHER, THANK YOU FOR. . .

....

....

HERE'S WHAT'S HAPPENING IN MY LIFE. . .

....

....

....

OTHER THINGS ON MY HEART THAT
I NEED TO SHARE WITH YOU, GOD. . .

....
....
....
....
....
....

I need. . .

....
....
....
....
....
....

Amen.

Thank You, Father,
for hearing my prayers.

GOALS *for this* MONTH

....
....
....
....
....
....
....
....

*Keep your lives free from the love of money and be
content with what you have, because God has said,
"Never will I leave you; never will I forsake you."*
HEBREWS 13:5 NIV

AUGUST 2022

S	M	T	W	T	F	S
		1	2	3	4	5	6
7	8	9	10	11	12	13
14	15	16	17	18	19	20
21	22	23	24	25	26	27
28	29	30	31			

When your net income is greater than expenses, month after month and year after year, good things are happening for you and your family. It means no cash flow problems, extra money on hand for emergencies, growing prosperity. You'll have healthy savings and a growing retirement account.

to-do list

- [ ]
- [ ]
- [ ]
- [ ]
- [ ]
- [ ]
- [ ]
- [ ]
- [ ]
- [ ]
- [ ]
- [ ]
- [ ]
- [ ]
- [ ]
- [ ]
- [ ]
- [ ]

SUNDAY, JULY 31

MONDAY, AUGUST 1

TUESDAY, AUGUST 2

WEDNESDAY, AUGUST 3

....
....
....
....
....

THURSDAY, AUGUST 4

....
....
....
....
....

FRIDAY, AUGUST 5

....
....
....
....
....

SATURDAY, AUGUST 6

....
....
....
....
....

to-do list

- [ ] ....
- [ ] ....
- [ ] ....
- [ ] ....
- [ ] ....
- [ ] ....
- [ ] ....
- [ ] ....
- [ ] ....
- [ ] ....
- [ ] ....
- [ ] ....
- [ ] ....
- [ ] ....
- [ ] ....
- [ ] ....

Wealth gained hastily will dwindle, but whoever gathers little by little will increase it.
PROVERBS 13:11 ESV

AUGUST 2022

S	M	T	W	T	F	S
		1	2	3	4	5	6
7	8	9	10	11	12	13
14	15	16	17	18	19	20
21	22	23	24	25	26	27
28	29	30	31			

When you need more income, seek it out—but beware of increasing your hours or stress. If a promotion or new job takes a while to gain, that's okay. Better to wait than to make a costly mistake.

to-do list

- [ ]
- [ ]
- [ ]
- [ ]
- [ ]
- [ ]
- [ ]
- [ ]
- [ ]
- [ ]
- [ ]
- [ ]
- [ ]
- [ ]
- [ ]
- [ ]
- [ ]
- [ ]
- [ ]

SUNDAY, AUGUST 7

MONDAY, AUGUST 8

TUESDAY, AUGUST 9

WEDNESDAY, AUGUST 10

THURSDAY, AUGUST 11

FRIDAY, AUGUST 12

SATURDAY, AUGUST 13

to-do list

- [ ]
- [ ]
- [ ]
- [ ]
- [ ]
- [ ]
- [ ]
- [ ]
- [ ]
- [ ]
- [ ]
- [ ]
- [ ]
- [ ]
- [ ]
- [ ]

Remember the LORD your God, for it is he who gives you the ability to produce wealth.
DEUTERONOMY 8:18 NIV

AUGUST 2022

S	M	T	W	T	F	S
	1	2	3	4	5	6
7	8	9	10	11	12	13
14	15	16	17	18	19	20
21	22	23	24	25	26	27
28	29	30	31			

The more you can reduce your monthly expenses, the more you'll have to put toward more important things. Christians have plenty of those.

to-do list

- ☐ ....
- ☐ ....
- ☐ ....
- ☐ ....
- ☐ ....
- ☐ ....
- ☐ ....
- ☐ ....
- ☐ ....
- ☐ ....
- ☐ ....
- ☐ ....
- ☐ ....
- ☐ ....
- ☐ ....
- ☐ ....
- ☐ ....
- ☐ ....
- ☐ ....

SUNDAY, AUGUST 14

MONDAY, AUGUST 15

TUESDAY, AUGUST 16

WEDNESDAY, AUGUST 17

to-do list

- [ ]
- [ ]
- [ ]
- [ ]
- [ ]
- [ ]
- [ ]
- [ ]
- [ ]
- [ ]
- [ ]
- [ ]
- [ ]
- [ ]
- [ ]
- [ ]

THURSDAY, AUGUST 18

FRIDAY, AUGUST 19

SATURDAY, AUGUST 20

"Won't you first sit down and estimate the cost to see if you have enough money?"
LUKE 14:28 NIV

AUGUST 2022

S	M	T	W	T	F	S
	1	2	3	4	5	6
7	8	9	10	11	12	13
14	15	16	17	18	19	20
21	22	23	24	25	26	27
28	29	30	31			

We all know that money and things can be very attractive to our human nature. We enjoy *seeing* nice things. As we prosper, we might enjoy *owning* such things. The apostle Paul's secret was to be content both when he possessed things and when they were lost due to wear and tear, accident, theft, imprisonment—or worse.

to-do list

- [ ]
- [ ]
- [ ]
- [ ]
- [ ]
- [ ]
- [ ]
- [ ]
- [ ]
- [ ]
- [ ]
- [ ]
- [ ]
- [ ]
- [ ]
- [ ]
- [ ]
- [ ]
- [ ]

SUNDAY, AUGUST 21

MONDAY, AUGUST 22

TUESDAY, AUGUST 23

WEDNESDAY, AUGUST 24

THURSDAY, AUGUST 25

FRIDAY, AUGUST 26

SATURDAY, AUGUST 27

to-do list

- [ ]
- [ ]
- [ ]
- [ ]
- [ ]
- [ ]
- [ ]
- [ ]
- [ ]
- [ ]
- [ ]
- [ ]
- [ ]
- [ ]
- [ ]
- [ ]

"I have not coveted anyone's silver or gold or clothing. You yourselves know that these hands of mine have supplied my own needs and the needs of my companions."
ACTS 20:33–34 NIV

AUGUST 2022

S	M	T	W	T	F	S
		1	2	3	4	5	6
7	8	9	10	11	12	13
14	15	16	17	18	19	20
21	22	23	24	25	26	27
28	29	30	31			

When you make a small financial mistake, don't ignore it. If you've just bought something you realize you can't afford, return or exchange it. If you've incurred a first-time overdraft charge, drop by your bank, apologize, promise it will never happen again, and ask, "This one time, is there any way this overdraft charge could be reversed?" It never hurts to ask.

to-do list

- [ ]
- [ ]
- [ ]
- [ ]
- [ ]
- [ ]
- [ ]
- [ ]
- [ ]
- [ ]
- [ ]
- [ ]
- [ ]
- [ ]
- [ ]
- [ ]
- [ ]
- [ ]

SUNDAY, AUGUST 28

MONDAY, AUGUST 29

TUESDAY, AUGUST 30

WEDNESDAY, AUGUST 31

THURSDAY, SEPTEMBER 1

FRIDAY, SEPTEMBER 2

SATURDAY, SEPTEMBER 3

to-do list

- [ ]
- [ ]
- [ ]
- [ ]
- [ ]
- [ ]
- [ ]
- [ ]
- [ ]
- [ ]
- [ ]
- [ ]
- [ ]
- [ ]
- [ ]
- [ ]

The rich rule over the poor, and the borrower is slave to the lender.
PROVERBS 22:7 NIV

SEPTEMBER 2022

SUNDAY	MONDAY	TUESDAY	WEDNESDAY
28	29	30	31
4	5 *Labor Day*	6	7
11	12	13	14
18	19	20	21
25	26	27	28

notes

THURSDAY	FRIDAY	SATURDAY
1	2	3
8	9	10
15	16	17
22	23	24
29 *First Day of Autumn*	30	1

·····································
·····································
·····································
·····································
·····································
·····································
·····································
·····································
·····································
·····································
·····································
·····································
·····································

AUGUST

S	M	T	W	T	F	S
	1	2	3	4	5	6
7	8	9	10	11	12	13
14	15	16	17	18	19	20
21	22	23	24	25	26	27
28	29	30	31			

OCTOBER

S	M	T	W	T	F	S
						1
2	3	4	5	6	7	8
9	10	11	12	13	14	15
16	17	18	19	20	21	22
23	24	25	26	27	28	29
30	31					

MY *September* LIFE MAP

GIVING BACK

*Never be lacking in zeal, but keep
your spiritual fervor, serving the Lord.*
ROMANS 12:11 NIV

Jesus rarely made statements that are easy to believe. Take His words, "You're far happier giving than getting" (Acts 20:35 MSG). Too good to be true? Well, actually, lots of scientifically backed research has documented this counterintuitive reality.

"Giving back" includes volunteer service, community leadership, financial contributions, and relational support. Among the many benefits that you'll enjoy are personal happiness, lowered stress, and an improved immune system. Givers report greater satisfaction with life, more meaning in life, more friends, and stronger relationships. They know they've helped to make others happier!

Want some more benefits to giving back? How about a more positive outlook on life, improved mental health, deeper contentment, higher self-esteem, and improved spiritual vitality. And don't forget the *eternal* rewards.

DEAR HEAVENLY FATHER, THANK YOU FOR. . .

HERE'S WHAT'S HAPPENING IN MY LIFE. . .

OTHER THINGS ON MY HEART THAT I NEED TO SHARE WITH YOU, GOD. . .

I need. . .

Amen.
Thank You, Father,
for hearing my prayers.

GOALS *for this* MONTH

*And this same God who takes care of me will
supply all your needs from his glorious riches,
which have been given to us in Christ Jesus.*
PHILIPPIANS 4:19 NLT

SEPTEMBER 2022

S	M	T	W	T	F	S
				1	2	3
4	5	6	7	8	9	10
11	12	13	14	15	16	17
18	19	20	21	22	23	24
25	26	27	28	29	30	

If your church has policies about who can serve when and where, be grateful—and do whatever you can to fulfill each requirement. Ask which volunteer opportunities are open, check out one or two ministries to find your best fit, and offer your services. God gifts every vibrant church with enough volunteers. Always make sure you are doing your part.

to-do list

☐ ....
☐ ....
☐ ....
☐ ....
☐ ....
☐ ....
☐ ....
☐ ....
☐ ....
☐ ....
☐ ....
☐ ....
☐ ....
☐ ....
☐ ....
☐ ....
☐ ....
☐ ....
☐ ....

SUNDAY, SEPTEMBER 4

MONDAY, SEPTEMBER 5   *Labor Day*

TUESDAY, SEPTEMBER 6

WEDNESDAY, SEPTEMBER 7

....
....
....
....
....

THURSDAY, SEPTEMBER 8

....
....
....
....
....

FRIDAY, SEPTEMBER 9

....
....
....
....
....

SATURDAY, SEPTEMBER 10

....
....
....
....
....

to-do list

- [ ] ....
- [ ] ....
- [ ] ....
- [ ] ....
- [ ] ....
- [ ] ....
- [ ] ....
- [ ] ....
- [ ] ....
- [ ] ....
- [ ] ....
- [ ] ....
- [ ] ....
- [ ] ....
- [ ] ....
- [ ] ....

Always give yourselves fully to the work of the Lord, because you know that your labor in the Lord is not in vain.
1 CORINTHIANS 15:58 NIV

SEPTEMBER 2022

S	M	T	W	T	F	S
				1	2	3
4	5	6	7	8	9	10
11	12	13	14	15	16	17
18	19	20	21	22	23	24
25	26	27	28	29	30	

Many churches get by on a tight budget. We might not think our own giving contributes that much, but joined with the regular gifts of others, the church is enabled to minister to its people and our community. What really matters is your decision to give regularly and cheerfully to God's work.

to-do list

☐ ....
☐ ....
☐ ....
☐ ....
☐ ....
☐ ....
☐ ....
☐ ....
☐ ....
☐ ....
☐ ....
☐ ....
☐ ....
☐ ....
☐ ....
☐ ....
☐ ....
☐ ....
☐ ....

SUNDAY, SEPTEMBER 11

MONDAY, SEPTEMBER 12

TUESDAY, SEPTEMBER 13

WEDNESDAY, SEPTEMBER 14

....
....
....
....
....

THURSDAY, SEPTEMBER 15

....
....
....
....
....

FRIDAY, SEPTEMBER 16

....
....
....
....
....

SATURDAY, SEPTEMBER 17

....
....
....
....
....

to-do list

☐ ....
☐ ....
☐ ....
☐ ....
☐ ....
☐ ....
☐ ....
☐ ....
☐ ....
☐ ....
☐ ....
☐ ....
☐ ....
☐ ....
☐ ....
☐ ....

*Each of you should give
what you have decided
in your heart to give,
not reluctantly or under
compulsion, for God
loves a cheerful giver.*
2 CORINTHIANS 9:7 NIV

SEPTEMBER 2022

S	M	T	W	T	F	S
				1	2	3
4	5	6	7	8	9	10
11	12	13	14	15	16	17
18	19	20	21	22	23	24
25	26	27	28	29	30	

Churches generally don't talk a lot about their benevolence funds. But they can be vital to many people. Why not ask your pastor if your church has one—and if it needs more donations to keep it strong.

to-do list

- [ ]
- [ ]
- [ ]
- [ ]
- [ ]
- [ ]
- [ ]
- [ ]
- [ ]
- [ ]
- [ ]
- [ ]
- [ ]
- [ ]
- [ ]
- [ ]
- [ ]
- [ ]
- [ ]

SUNDAY, SEPTEMBER 18

MONDAY, SEPTEMBER 19

TUESDAY, SEPTEMBER 20

WEDNESDAY, SEPTEMBER 21

....

....

....

....

....

THURSDAY, SEPTEMBER 22
First Day of Autumn

....

....

....

....

FRIDAY, SEPTEMBER 23

....

....

....

....

....

SATURDAY, SEPTEMBER 24

....

....

....

....

....

to-do list

☐ ....
☐ ....
☐ ....
☐ ....
☐ ....
☐ ....
☐ ....
☐ ....
☐ ....
☐ ....
☐ ....
☐ ....
☐ ....
☐ ....
☐ ....
☐ ....
☐ ....

*"In everything I did,
I showed you that by
this kind of hard work
we must help the weak,
remembering the words
the Lord Jesus himself
said: 'It is more blessed
to give than to receive.'"*
ACTS 20:35 NIV

SEPTEMBER 2022

S	M	T	W	T	F	S
				1	2	3
4	5	6	7	8	9	10
11	12	13	14	15	16	17
18	19	20	21	22	23	24
25	26	27	28	29	30	

As God leads you, sign up to receive the newsletters from your favorite missionaries. Be sure to connect with them via email and social media. As you get to know each other better, contribute funds via your church for their support. Such financial gifts are "acceptable and pleasing to God" (Philippians 4:18 NLT).

to-do list

- [ ]
- [ ]
- [ ]
- [ ]
- [ ]
- [ ]
- [ ]
- [ ]
- [ ]
- [ ]
- [ ]
- [ ]
- [ ]
- [ ]
- [ ]
- [ ]
- [ ]
- [ ]
- [ ]

SUNDAY, SEPTEMBER 25

MONDAY, SEPTEMBER 26

TUESDAY, SEPTEMBER 27

WEDNESDAY, SEPTEMBER 28

....
....
....
....
....

THURSDAY, SEPTEMBER 29

....
....
....
....
....

FRIDAY, SEPTEMBER 30

....
....
....
....
....

SATURDAY, OCTOBER 1

....
....
....
....

to-do list

☐ ....
☐ ....
☐ ....
☐ ....
☐ ....
☐ ....
☐ ....
☐ ....
☐ ....
☐ ....
☐ ....
☐ ....
☐ ....
☐ ....
☐ ....

These women were helping to support [Jesus and the Twelve] out of their own means.
LUKE 8:3 NIV

OCTOBER 2022

SUNDAY	MONDAY	TUESDAY	WEDNESDAY
25	26	27	28
2	3	4	5
9	10 *Columbus Day*	11	12
16	17	18	19
23 30	24 31 *Halloween*	25	26

notes

THURSDAY	FRIDAY	SATURDAY
29	30	1
6	7	8
13	14	15
20	21	22
27	28	29

....
....
....
....
....
....
....
....
....
....
....
....
....

SEPTEMBER

S	M	T	W	T	F	S
				1	2	3
4	5	6	7	8	9	10
11	12	13	14	15	16	17
18	19	20	21	22	23	24
25	26	27	28	29	30	

NOVEMBER

S	M	T	W	T	F	S
		1	2	3	4	5
6	7	8	9	10	11	12
13	14	15	16	17	18	19
20	21	22	23	24	25	26
27	28	29	30			

CHURCH ATTENDANCE

You will know how people ought to conduct themselves in God's household, which is the church of the living God, the pillar and foundation of the truth.
1 TIMOTHY 3:15 NIV

Every man who follows Jesus Christ is a member of God's kingdom, God's family, and God's church. The last two chapters of Revelation celebrate the future realities of all three. Here and now, though, Jesus calls us to be active members of a local expression of His church.

We sometimes forget that the church is the Lord's idea. Jesus founded it so His followers could more effectively make disciples by teaching His commandments, offering water baptism, and reminding them that He is "with you always, to the very end of the age" (Matthew 28:20 NIV).

Some denominations carry a rich sense of history. Some follow the church calendar and use liturgy. Some provide a deep theological tradition. Some support robust ministries locally, regionally, nationally, or overseas. Some proclaim the Gospel in some form every Sunday.

The more you love Jesus Christ's bride, the church, the more you love Jesus Himself.

DEAR HEAVENLY FATHER, THANK YOU FOR. . .

....

....

....

HERE'S WHAT'S HAPPENING IN MY LIFE. . .

....

....

....

OTHER THINGS ON MY HEART THAT
I NEED TO SHARE WITH YOU, GOD. . .

....
....
....
....
....
....

I need. . .

....
....
....
....
....
....
....

Amen.
Thank You, Father,
for hearing my prayers.

GOALS *for this* MONTH

....
....
....
....
....
....
....
....

You are a chosen people, a royal priesthood, a holy nation,
God's special possession, that you may declare the praises
of him who called you out of darkness into his wonderful light.
1 PETER 2:9 NIV

OCTOBER 2022

S	M	T	W	T	F	S
						1
2	3	4	5	6	7	8
9	10	11	12	13	14	15
16	17	18	19	20	21	22
23	24	25	26	27	28	29
30	31					

Each denomination and Christian group has gifts for the rest of the church. What a joy to be blessed—directly or indirectly—by some of those gifts. Conversely, every group has a few customs or traditions that may feel peculiar to you. That's okay. In most cases, it's not wrong, just different.

to-do list

- [ ]
- [ ]
- [ ]
- [ ]
- [ ]
- [ ]
- [ ]
- [ ]
- [ ]
- [ ]
- [ ]
- [ ]
- [ ]
- [ ]
- [ ]
- [ ]
- [ ]
- [ ]
- [ ]

SUNDAY, OCTOBER 2

MONDAY, OCTOBER 3

TUESDAY, OCTOBER 4

WEDNESDAY, OCTOBER 5

....
....
....
....
....

THURSDAY, OCTOBER 6

....
....
....
....
....

FRIDAY, OCTOBER 7

....
....
....
....
....

SATURDAY, OCTOBER 8

....
....
....
....
....

to-do list

- [ ] ....
- [ ] ....
- [ ] ....
- [ ] ....
- [ ] ....
- [ ] ....
- [ ] ....
- [ ] ....
- [ ] ....
- [ ] ....
- [ ] ....
- [ ] ....
- [ ] ....
- [ ] ....
- [ ] ....
- [ ] ....

In Christ we, though many, form one body, and each member belongs to all the others.
ROMANS 12:5 NIV

OCTOBER 2022

S	M	T	W	T	F	S
						1
2	3	4	5	6	7	8
9	10	11	12	13	14	15
16	17	18	19	20	21	22
23	24	25	26	27	28	29
30	31					

Think of the larger church—the overall "body of Christ"—like a tree. It has a lot of branches that stretch around the world and roots that go down through the centuries. Today, choosing a local church is both an objective issue (Is it biblical?) and a subjective matter (Is it a good fit?). In other words, you have a lot of freedom—so enjoy the process.

to-do list

- [ ] ....
- [ ] ....
- [ ] ....
- [ ] ....
- [ ] ....
- [ ] ....
- [ ] ....
- [ ] ....
- [ ] ....
- [ ] ....
- [ ] ....
- [ ] ....
- [ ] ....
- [ ] ....
- [ ] ....
- [ ] ....
- [ ] ....
- [ ] ....
- [ ] ....

SUNDAY, OCTOBER 9

MONDAY, OCTOBER 10 *Columbus Day*

TUESDAY, OCTOBER 11

WEDNESDAY, OCTOBER 12

THURSDAY, OCTOBER 13

FRIDAY, OCTOBER 14

SATURDAY, OCTOBER 15

to-do list

☐
☐
☐
☐
☐
☐
☐
☐
☐
☐
☐
☐
☐
☐
☐
☐

*Preach the word;
be prepared in season and
out of season; correct,
rebuke and encourage—
with great patience and
careful instruction.*
2 TIMOTHY 4:2 NIV

OCTOBER 2022

S	M	T	W	T	F	S
						1
2	3	4	5	6	7	8
9	10	11	12	13	14	15
16	17	18	19	20	21	22
23	24	25	26	27	28	29
30	31					

International evangelist Luis Palau has said, "In 1 Corinthians 12:26 [NIV] we read, 'If one part suffers, every part suffers with it; if one part is honored, every part rejoices with it.' How you relate or fail to relate to the body of Christ directly affects other Christians. We need each other!"

to-do list

- [ ] ....
- [ ] ....
- [ ] ....
- [ ] ....
- [ ] ....
- [ ] ....
- [ ] ....
- [ ] ....
- [ ] ....
- [ ] ....
- [ ] ....
- [ ] ....
- [ ] ....
- [ ] ....
- [ ] ....
- [ ] ....
- [ ] ....
- [ ] ....

SUNDAY, OCTOBER 16

MONDAY, OCTOBER 17

TUESDAY, OCTOBER 18

WEDNESDAY, OCTOBER 19

....
....
....
....
....

THURSDAY, OCTOBER 20

....
....
....
....
....

FRIDAY, OCTOBER 21

....
....
....
....
....

SATURDAY, OCTOBER 22

....
....
....
....
....

to-do list

- [ ] ....
- [ ] ....
- [ ] ....
- [ ] ....
- [ ] ....
- [ ] ....
- [ ] ....
- [ ] ....
- [ ] ....
- [ ] ....
- [ ] ....
- [ ] ....
- [ ] ....
- [ ] ....
- [ ] ....
- [ ] ....

*Then the church. . .enjoyed
a time of peace and was
strengthened. Living in
the fear of the Lord and
encouraged by the Holy
Spirit, it increased
in numbers.*
ACTS 9:31 NIV

OCTOBER 2022

S	M	T	W	T	F	S
						1
2	3	4	5	6	7	8
9	10	11	12	13	14	15
16	17	18	19	20	21	22
23	24	25	26	27	28	29
30	31					

After visiting a range of churches, it's important to decide which most appeal to you. Criteria include preaching, music, ministries, theological compatibility, and open-handedness. The latter is a church's willingness to allow for differences on second- and third-level doctrinal matters. But never relax on the core of orthodoxy.

to-do list

☐ ....
☐ ....
☐ ....
☐ ....
☐ ....
☐ ....
☐ ....
☐ ....
☐ ....
☐ ....
☐ ....
☐ ....
☐ ....
☐ ....
☐ ....
☐ ....
☐ ....
☐ ....

SUNDAY, OCTOBER 23

MONDAY, OCTOBER 24

TUESDAY, OCTOBER 25

WEDNESDAY, OCTOBER 26

....
....
....
....
....

THURSDAY, OCTOBER 27

....
....
....
....
....

FRIDAY, OCTOBER 28

....
....
....
....
....

SATURDAY, OCTOBER 29

....
....
....
....
....

to-do list

- [ ] ....
- [ ] ....
- [ ] ....
- [ ] ....
- [ ] ....
- [ ] ....
- [ ] ....
- [ ] ....
- [ ] ....
- [ ] ....
- [ ] ....
- [ ] ....
- [ ] ....
- [ ] ....
- [ ] ....
- [ ] ....
- [ ] ....

Although I was very eager to write to you about the salvation we share, I felt compelled to write and urge you to contend for the faith that was once for all entrusted to God's holy people.
JUDE 3 NIV

NOVEMBER 2022

SUNDAY	MONDAY	TUESDAY	WEDNESDAY
30	31	1	2
6 *Daylight Saving Time Ends*	7	8 *Election Day*	9
13	14	15	16
20	21	22	23
27	28	29	30

notes

THURSDAY	FRIDAY	SATURDAY
3	4	5
10	11 *Veterans Day*	12
17	18	19
24 *Thanksgiving Day*	25	26
1	2	3

....
....
....
....
....
....
....
....
....
....
....
....
....

OCTOBER

S	M	T	W	T	F	S
						1
2	3	4	5	6	7	8
9	10	11	12	13	14	15
16	17	18	19	20	21	22
23	24	25	26	27	28	29
30	31					

DECEMBER

S	M	T	W	T	F	S
				1	2	3
4	5	6	7	8	9	10
11	12	13	14	15	16	17
18	19	20	21	22	23	24
25	26	27	28	29	30	31

KNOWING GOD

"Yours, LORD, is the greatness and the power and
the glory and the majesty and the splendor,
for everything in heaven and earth is yours."
1 CHRONICLES 29:11 NIV

No other question is more important than "Who is God?"

Get this one right—and experience who He is each day—and you'll enjoy life to the full. We see this truth in Deuteronomy 7:12–13; Psalm 16:2; John 10:10; James 1:17; and plenty of other places throughout the Bible.

Pastor and author A. W. Tozer wrote, "The man who comes to a right belief about God is relieved of ten thousand temporal problems, for he sees at once that these have to do with matters which at the most cannot concern him for very long." What hope!

DEAR HEAVENLY FATHER, THANK YOU FOR. . .

HERE'S WHAT'S HAPPENING IN MY LIFE. . .

I need. . .

....
....
....
....
....
....

OTHER THINGS ON MY HEART THAT
I NEED TO SHARE WITH YOU, GOD. . .

....
....
....
....
....
....

Amen.
Thank You, Father,
for hearing my prayers.

GOALS *for this* MONTH

....
....
....
....
....
....
....
....

*"For Yours is the kingdom and the
power and the glory forever."*
MATTHEW 6:13 NKJV

NOVEMBER 2022

S	M	T	W	T	F	S
		1	2	3	4	5
6	7	8	9	10	11	12
13	14	15	16	17	18	19
20	21	22	23	24	25	26
27	28	29	30			

Does God's powerful presence permeate every millisecond and millimeter of your life? Yes, whether you realize that or not. You're never alone. And you're never powerless. God is with you, asking, "What do you want Me to do for you?" Call out to Him today.

to-do list

- [ ] ....
- [ ] ....
- [ ] ....
- [ ] ....
- [ ] ....
- [ ] ....
- [ ] ....
- [ ] ....
- [ ] ....
- [ ] ....
- [ ] ....
- [ ] ....
- [ ] ....
- [ ] ....
- [ ] ....
- [ ] ....
- [ ] ....
- [ ] ....
- [ ] ....

SUNDAY, OCTOBER 30

MONDAY, OCTOBER 31   *Halloween*

TUESDAY, NOVEMBER 1

WEDNESDAY, NOVEMBER 2

THURSDAY, NOVEMBER 3

FRIDAY, NOVEMBER 4

SATURDAY, NOVEMBER 5

to-do list

- [ ]
- [ ]
- [ ]
- [ ]
- [ ]
- [ ]
- [ ]
- [ ]
- [ ]
- [ ]
- [ ]
- [ ]
- [ ]
- [ ]
- [ ]
- [ ]

"Sovereign Lord. . .you
made the heavens and
the earth and the sea,
and everything in them."
ACTS 4:24 NIV

NOVEMBER 2022

S	M	T	W	T	F	S
		1	2	3	4	5
6	7	8	9	10	11	12
13	14	15	16	17	18	19
20	21	22	23	24	25	26
27	28	29	30			

Stories of heroes of the faith often demonstrate God's invisible hand at work, guiding and providing. He assured Isaiah, "I make known the end from the beginning, from ancient times, what is still to come. I say, 'My purpose will stand, and I will do all that I please' " (Isaiah 46:10 NIV).

to-do list

- [ ] ....
- [ ] ....
- [ ] ....
- [ ] ....
- [ ] ....
- [ ] ....
- [ ] ....
- [ ] ....
- [ ] ....
- [ ] ....
- [ ] ....
- [ ] ....
- [ ] ....
- [ ] ....
- [ ] ....
- [ ] ....
- [ ] ....
- [ ] ....
- [ ] ....

SUNDAY, NOVEMBER 6
Daylight Saving Time Ends

MONDAY, NOVEMBER 7

TUESDAY, NOVEMBER 8 *Election Day*

WEDNESDAY, NOVEMBER 9

....
....
....
....
....

THURSDAY, NOVEMBER 10

....
....
....
....
....

FRIDAY, NOVEMBER 11   *Veterans Day*

....
....
....
....
....

SATURDAY, NOVEMBER 12

....
....
....
....
....

to-do list

- [ ] ....
- [ ] ....
- [ ] ....
- [ ] ....
- [ ] ....
- [ ] ....
- [ ] ....
- [ ] ....
- [ ] ....
- [ ] ....
- [ ] ....
- [ ] ....
- [ ] ....
- [ ] ....
- [ ] ....
- [ ] ....

*"You gave me life and
showed me kindness,
and in your providence
watched over my spirit."*
JOB 10:12 NIV

NOVEMBER 2022

S	M	T	W	T	F	S
		1	2	3	4	5
6	7	8	9	10	11	12
13	14	15	16	17	18	19
20	21	22	23	24	25	26
27	28	29	30			

Holy and its synonyms appear more than sixteen hundred times throughout the Bible. It quickly becomes clear that God is holy, people aren't, God expects us to be holy, and we can't be holy without His divine transformation.

to-do list

- [ ]
- [ ]
- [ ]
- [ ]
- [ ]
- [ ]
- [ ]
- [ ]
- [ ]
- [ ]
- [ ]
- [ ]
- [ ]
- [ ]
- [ ]
- [ ]
- [ ]
- [ ]
- [ ]

SUNDAY, NOVEMBER 13

MONDAY, NOVEMBER 14

TUESDAY, NOVEMBER 15

WEDNESDAY, NOVEMBER 16

THURSDAY, NOVEMBER 17

FRIDAY, NOVEMBER 18

SATURDAY, NOVEMBER 19

to-do list

☐
☐
☐
☐
☐
☐
☐
☐
☐
☐
☐
☐
☐
☐
☐
☐

Therefore, since we have these promises, dear friends, let us purify ourselves from everything that contaminates body and spirit, perfecting holiness out of reverence for God.
2 CORINTHIANS 7:1 NIV

NOVEMBER 2022

S	M	T	W	T	F	S
		1	2	3	4	5
6	7	8	9	10	11	12
13	14	15	16	17	18	19
20	21	22	23	24	25	26
27	28	29	30			

Remember the Lord's sacred name, YHWH? Here's the first part of how God Himself defines it: "The LORD, the LORD, the compassionate and gracious God, slow to anger, abounding in love and faithfulness, maintaining love to thousands, and forgiving wickedness, rebellion and sin" (Exodus 34:5–7 NIV). Did you notice that "love" appears twice in that statement?

to-do list

- [ ]
- [ ]
- [ ]
- [ ]
- [ ]
- [ ]
- [ ]
- [ ]
- [ ]
- [ ]
- [ ]
- [ ]
- [ ]
- [ ]
- [ ]
- [ ]
- [ ]
- [ ]
- [ ]

SUNDAY, NOVEMBER 20

MONDAY, NOVEMBER 21

TUESDAY, NOVEMBER 22

WEDNESDAY, NOVEMBER 23

....
....
....
....
....

THURSDAY, NOVEMBER 24
Thanksgiving Day

....
....
....
....

FRIDAY, NOVEMBER 25

....
....
....
....
....

SATURDAY, NOVEMBER 26

....
....
....
....
....

to-do list

- [ ] ....
- [ ] ....
- [ ] ....
- [ ] ....
- [ ] ....
- [ ] ....
- [ ] ....
- [ ] ....
- [ ] ....
- [ ] ....
- [ ] ....
- [ ] ....
- [ ] ....
- [ ] ....
- [ ] ....
- [ ] ....
- [ ] ....

God's love has been poured out into our hearts through the Holy Spirit, who has been given to us.
ROMANS 5:5 NIV

NOVEMBER 2022

S	M	T	W	T	F	S
		1	2	3	4	5
6	7	8	9	10	11	12
13	14	15	16	17	18	19
20	21	22	23	24	25	26
27	28	29	30			

None of us knows a millionth of one percent of everything that's true and right and important and life changing. So why in the world are we tempted to think we know better than God? Not a chance!

to-do list

- [ ]
- [ ]
- [ ]
- [ ]
- [ ]
- [ ]
- [ ]
- [ ]
- [ ]
- [ ]
- [ ]
- [ ]
- [ ]
- [ ]
- [ ]
- [ ]
- [ ]
- [ ]

SUNDAY, NOVEMBER 27

MONDAY, NOVEMBER 28

TUESDAY, NOVEMBER 29

WEDNESDAY, NOVEMBER 30

....
....
....
....
....

THURSDAY, DECEMBER 1

....
....
....
....
....

FRIDAY, DECEMBER 2

....
....
....
....
....

SATURDAY, DECEMBER 3

....
....
....
....
....

to-do list

- [ ] ....
- [ ] ....
- [ ] ....
- [ ] ....
- [ ] ....
- [ ] ....
- [ ] ....
- [ ] ....
- [ ] ....
- [ ] ....
- [ ] ....
- [ ] ....
- [ ] ....
- [ ] ....
- [ ] ....
- [ ] ....

*"For my thoughts are not
your thoughts, neither
are your ways my ways,"
declares the LORD.*
ISAIAH 55:8 NIV

DECEMBER 2022

SUNDAY	MONDAY	TUESDAY	WEDNESDAY
27	28	29	30
4	5	6	7
11	12	13	14
18 *Hanukkah Begins at Sundown*	19	20	21 *First Day of Winter*
25 *Christmas Day*	26	27	28

notes

THURSDAY	FRIDAY	SATURDAY
1	2	3
8	9	10
15	16	17
22	23	24 *Christmas Eve*
29	30	31 *New Year's Eve*

....
....
....
....
....
....
....
....
....
....
....
....
....

NOVEMBER

S	M	T	W	T	F	S
		1	2	3	4	5
6	7	8	9	10	11	12
13	14	15	16	17	18	19
20	21	22	23	24	25	26
27	28	29	30			

JANUARY

S	M	T	W	T	F	S
1	2	3	4	5	6	7
8	9	10	11	12	13	14
15	16	17	18	19	20	21
22	23	24	25	26	27	28
29	30	31				

FINISHING WELL

[Anna] came along just as Simeon was talking with Mary and Joseph, and she began praising God. She talked about the child to everyone who had been waiting expectantly for God to rescue Jerusalem.
LUKE 2:38 NLT

There's no more important decision than the choice to live for God your whole life. This commitment can include your spouse, your family, and your fellow church members.

In Jesus' time, Simeon had God's promise that he would not die until he saw the Messiah. It seems Anna had no such guarantee, but like many others, she knew the time of the Messiah's coming was near. While these two devout people waited, they lived righteously, walking with God in obedience and worshipping Him with all their hearts.

As Mary and Joseph entered the temple with baby Jesus cradled in their arms, they looked like any other faithful couple fulfilling their duty to God. But to an old man and an old woman led by the Holy Spirit, this little family stood out like a beacon. They were welcomed to God's house as no family had ever been greeted before.

Anna and Simeon served God their whole lives. They ended well—and with a unique blessing.

DEAR HEAVENLY FATHER, THANK YOU FOR. . .

HERE'S WHAT'S HAPPENING IN MY LIFE. . .

OTHER THINGS ON MY HEART THAT
I NEED TO SHARE WITH YOU, GOD. . .

I need. . .

Amen.
Thank You, Father,
for hearing my prayers.

GOALS *for this* MONTH

*Listen to advice and accept discipline,
and at the end you will be counted among the wise.*
PROVERBS 19:20 NIV

DECEMBER 2022

S	M	T	W	T	F	S
				1	2	3
4	5	6	7	8	9	10
11	12	13	14	15	16	17
18	19	20	21	22	23	24
25	26	27	28	29	30	31

Among his many creditable behaviors, Joseph—the husband of Mary—believed what the Lord revealed to him in a series of dreams, no matter how incredible those revelations seemed. Each time, Joseph quickly translated his belief into action, at great personal cost.

to-do list

- [ ]
- [ ]
- [ ]
- [ ]
- [ ]
- [ ]
- [ ]
- [ ]
- [ ]
- [ ]
- [ ]
- [ ]
- [ ]
- [ ]
- [ ]
- [ ]
- [ ]
- [ ]

SUNDAY, DECEMBER 4

MONDAY, DECEMBER 5

TUESDAY, DECEMBER 6

WEDNESDAY, DECEMBER 7

....
....
....
....
....

THURSDAY, DECEMBER 8

....
....
....
....
....

FRIDAY, DECEMBER 9

....
....
....
....
....

SATURDAY, DECEMBER 10

....
....
....
....
....

to-do list

- [ ] ....
- [ ] ....
- [ ] ....
- [ ] ....
- [ ] ....
- [ ] ....
- [ ] ....
- [ ] ....
- [ ] ....
- [ ] ....
- [ ] ....
- [ ] ....
- [ ] ....
- [ ] ....
- [ ] ....
- [ ] ....
- [ ] ....

*When Joseph woke up,
he did what the angel
of the Lord had
commanded him and took
Mary home as his wife.*
MATTHEW 1:24 NIV

DECEMBER 2022

S	M	T	W	T	F	S
				1	2	3
4	5	6	7	8	9	10
11	12	13	14	15	16	17
18	19	20	21	22	23	24
25	26	27	28	29	30	31

Timothy was young enough to have his ministry questioned. But he was also mature enough in his faith to be entrusted with the spiritual leadership of the church in a rather large city. Not all of us enjoy a rich spiritual heritage like Timothy. But each of us can choose to be an example of godliness. That's good for you and everyone around you.

to-do list

☐ ....
☐ ....
☐ ....
☐ ....
☐ ....
☐ ....
☐ ....
☐ ....
☐ ....
☐ ....
☐ ....
☐ ....
☐ ....
☐ ....
☐ ....
☐ ....
☐ ....
☐ ....
☐ ....

SUNDAY, DECEMBER 11

MONDAY, DECEMBER 12

TUESDAY, DECEMBER 13

WEDNESDAY, DECEMBER 14

....
....
....
....
....

THURSDAY, DECEMBER 15

....
....
....
....
....

FRIDAY, DECEMBER 16

....
....
....
....
....

SATURDAY, DECEMBER 17

....
....
....
....
....

to-do list

☐ ....
☐ ....
☐ ....
☐ ....
☐ ....
☐ ....
☐ ....
☐ ....
☐ ....
☐ ....
☐ ....
☐ ....
☐ ....
☐ ....
☐ ....
☐ ....

Don't let anyone look down on you because you are young, but set an example for the believers in speech, in conduct, in love, in faith and in purity.
1 TIMOTHY 4:12 NIV

DECEMBER 2022

S	M	T	W	T	F	S
				1	2	3
4	5	6	7	8	9	10
11	12	13	14	15	16	17
18	19	20	21	22	23	24
25	26	27	28	29	30	31

Despite his impressive credentials, Apollos never assumed he knew it all. He humbled himself to accept the wise guidance of Priscilla and Aquila, and his ministry grew accordingly. Apollos is a stellar example of a Christian committed to lifelong learning. Are you?

to-do list

- [ ]
- [ ]
- [ ]
- [ ]
- [ ]
- [ ]
- [ ]
- [ ]
- [ ]
- [ ]
- [ ]
- [ ]
- [ ]
- [ ]
- [ ]
- [ ]
- [ ]
- [ ]

SUNDAY, DECEMBER 18
Hanukkah Begins at Sundown

MONDAY, DECEMBER 19

TUESDAY, DECEMBER 20

WEDNESDAY, DECEMBER 21
First Day of Winter

THURSDAY, DECEMBER 22

FRIDAY, DECEMBER 23

SATURDAY, DECEMBER 24
Christmas Eve

to-do list

- [ ]
- [ ]
- [ ]
- [ ]
- [ ]
- [ ]
- [ ]
- [ ]
- [ ]
- [ ]
- [ ]
- [ ]
- [ ]
- [ ]
- [ ]
- [ ]

[Apollos] began to speak boldly in the synagogue. When Priscilla and Aquila heard him, they invited him to their home and explained to him the way of God more adequately.
ACTS 18:26 NIV

DECEMBER 2022

S	M	T	W	T	F	S
				1	2	3
4	5	6	7	8	9	10
11	12	13	14	15	16	17
18	19	20	21	22	23	24
25	26	27	28	29	30	31

The apostle Paul sent Titus on numerous mission trips around the Mediterranean. But first, Paul took Titus to the Jerusalem Council (Acts 15:2; Galatians 2:3). There he could be mentored not just by Paul, but by Barnabas, Peter, James, and others. No matter how much life and ministry experience we accumulate, we always benefit from mentors in our lives.

to-do list

- [ ]
- [ ]
- [ ]
- [ ]
- [ ]
- [ ]
- [ ]
- [ ]
- [ ]
- [ ]
- [ ]
- [ ]
- [ ]
- [ ]
- [ ]
- [ ]
- [ ]
- [ ]
- [ ]

SUNDAY, DECEMBER 25   *Christmas Day*

MONDAY, DECEMBER 26

TUESDAY, DECEMBER 27

WEDNESDAY, DECEMBER 28

THURSDAY, DECEMBER 29

FRIDAY, DECEMBER 30

SATURDAY, DECEMBER 31
New Year's Eve

The reason I left you in Crete was that you might put in order what was left unfinished and appoint elders in every town, as I directed you.
TITUS 1:5 NIV

CONTACTS

Name:

Address:

Phone: Cell:

Email:

Name:

Address:

Phone: Cell:

Email:

Name:

Address:

Phone: Cell:

Email:

Name:

Address:

Phone: Cell:

Email:

Name:

Address:

Phone: Cell:

Email:

CONTACTS

Name:

Address:

Phone: Cell:

Email:

Name:

Address:

Phone: Cell:

Email:

Name:

Address:

Phone: Cell:

Email:

Name:

Address:

Phone: Cell:

Email:

Name:

Address:

Phone: Cell:

Email:

CONTACTS

Name:

Address:

Phone: Cell:

Email:

Name:

Address:

Phone: Cell:

Email:

Name:

Address:

Phone: Cell:

Email:

Name:

Address:

Phone: Cell:

Email:

Name:

Address:

Phone: Cell:

Email:

CONTACTS

Name:

Address:

Phone: Cell:

Email:

Name:

Address:

Phone: Cell:

Email:

Name:

Address:

Phone: Cell:

Email:

Name:

Address:

Phone: Cell:

Email:

Name:

Address:

Phone: Cell:

Email:

CONTACTS

Name:

Address:

Phone: Cell:

Email:

Name:

Address:

Phone: Cell:

Email:

Name:

Address:

Phone: Cell:

Email:

Name:

Address:

Phone: Cell:

Email:

Name:

Address:

Phone: Cell:

Email:

CONTACTS

Name:

Address:

Phone: Cell:

Email:

Name:

Address:

Phone: Cell:

Email:

Name:

Address:

Phone: Cell:

Email:

Name:

Address:

Phone: Cell:

Email:

Name:

Address:

Phone: Cell:

Email:

NOTES & IDEAS

NOTES & IDEAS

NOTES & IDEAS

NOTES & IDEAS

NOTES & IDEAS

NOTES & IDEAS

NOTES & IDEAS

NOTES & IDEAS

NOTES & IDEAS

NOTES & IDEAS

2023

JANUARY
S	M	T	W	T	F	S
1	2	3	4	5	6	7
8	9	10	11	12	13	14
15	16	17	18	19	20	21
22	23	24	25	26	27	28
29	30	31				

FEBRUARY
S	M	T	W	T	F	S
			1	2	3	4
5	6	7	8	9	10	11
12	13	14	15	16	17	18
19	20	21	22	23	24	25
26	27	28				

MARCH
S	M	T	W	T	F	S
			1	2	3	4
5	6	7	8	9	10	11
12	13	14	15	16	17	18
19	20	21	22	23	24	25
26	27	28	29	30	31	

APRIL
S	M	T	W	T	F	S
						1
2	3	4	5	6	7	8
9	10	11	12	13	14	15
16	17	18	19	20	21	22
23	24	25	26	27	28	29
30						

MAY
S	M	T	W	T	F	S
	1	2	3	4	5	6
7	8	9	10	11	12	13
14	15	16	17	18	19	20
21	22	23	24	25	26	27
28	29	30	31			

JUNE
S	M	T	W	T	F	S
				1	2	3
4	5	6	7	8	9	10
11	12	13	14	15	16	17
18	19	20	21	22	23	24
25	26	27	28	29	30	

JULY
S	M	T	W	T	F	S
						1
2	3	4	5	6	7	8
9	10	11	12	13	14	15
16	17	18	19	20	21	22
23	24	25	26	27	28	29
30	31					

AUGUST
S	M	T	W	T	F	S
		1	2	3	4	5
6	7	8	9	10	11	12
13	14	15	16	17	18	19
20	21	22	23	24	25	26
27	28	29	30	31		

SEPTEMBER
S	M	T	W	T	F	S
					1	2
3	4	5	6	7	8	9
10	11	12	13	14	15	16
17	18	19	20	21	22	23
24	25	26	27	28	29	30

OCTOBER
S	M	T	W	T	F	S
1	2	3	4	5	6	7
8	9	10	11	12	13	14
15	16	17	18	19	20	21
22	23	24	25	26	27	28
29	30	31				

NOVEMBER
S	M	T	W	T	F	S
			1	2	3	4
5	6	7	8	9	10	11
12	13	14	15	16	17	18
19	20	21	22	23	24	25
26	27	28	29	30		

DECEMBER
S	M	T	W	T	F	S
					1	2
3	4	5	6	7	8	9
10	11	12	13	14	15	16
17	18	19	20	21	22	23
24	25	26	27	28	29	30
31						

2024

JANUARY
S	M	T	W	T	F	S
	1	2	3	4	5	6
7	8	9	10	11	12	13
14	15	16	17	18	19	20
21	22	23	24	25	26	27
28	29	30	31			

FEBRUARY
S	M	T	W	T	F	S
				1	2	3
4	5	6	7	8	9	10
11	12	13	14	15	16	17
18	19	20	21	22	23	24
25	26	27	28	29		

MARCH
S	M	T	W	T	F	S
					1	2
3	4	5	6	7	8	9
10	11	12	13	14	15	16
17	18	19	20	21	22	23
24	25	26	27	28	29	30
31						

APRIL
S	M	T	W	T	F	S
	1	2	3	4	5	6
7	8	9	10	11	12	13
14	15	16	17	18	19	20
21	22	23	24	25	26	27
28	29	30				

MAY
S	M	T	W	T	F	S
			1	2	3	4
5	6	7	8	9	10	11
12	13	14	15	16	17	18
19	20	21	22	23	24	25
26	27	28	29	30	31	

JUNE
S	M	T	W	T	F	S
						1
2	3	4	5	6	7	8
9	10	11	12	13	14	15
16	17	18	19	20	21	22
23	24	25	26	27	28	29
30						

JULY
S	M	T	W	T	F	S
	1	2	3	4	5	6
7	8	9	10	11	12	13
14	15	16	17	18	19	20
21	22	23	24	25	26	27
28	29	30	31			

AUGUST
S	M	T	W	T	F	S
				1	2	3
4	5	6	7	8	9	10
11	12	13	14	15	16	17
18	19	20	21	22	23	24
25	26	27	28	29	30	31

SEPTEMBER
S	M	T	W	T	F	S
1	2	3	4	5	6	7
8	9	10	11	12	13	14
15	16	17	18	19	20	21
22	23	24	25	26	27	28
29	30					

OCTOBER
S	M	T	W	T	F	S
		1	2	3	4	5
6	7	8	9	10	11	12
13	14	15	16	17	18	19
20	21	22	23	24	25	26
27	28	29	30	31		

NOVEMBER
S	M	T	W	T	F	S
					1	2
3	4	5	6	7	8	9
10	11	12	13	14	15	16
17	18	19	20	21	22	23
24	25	26	27	28	29	30

DECEMBER
S	M	T	W	T	F	S
1	2	3	4	5	6	7
8	9	10	11	12	13	14
15	16	17	18	19	20	21
22	23	24	25	26	27	28
29	30	31				